J Spencer Kinard

THE WORTH OF A SMILE

Spoken Words
for
Daily Living

by
J. Spencer Kinard

PRENTICE-HALL, INC.
Englewood Cliffs, N.J.

THE WORTH OF A SMILE

Spoken Words for Daily Living

by
J. Spencer Kinard

PRENTICE-HALL, INC.
Englewood Cliffs, N.J.

THE WORTH OF A SMILE:
Spoken Words for Daily Living by J. Spencer Kinard

Copyright © 1976 by J. Spencer Kinard

Printed in the United States of America
Prentice-Hall International, Inc., London
Prentice-Hall of Australia, Pty. Ltd., Sydney
Prentice-Hall of Canada, Ltd., Toronto
Prentice-Hall of India Private Ltd., New Delhi
Prentice-Hall of Japan, Inc., Tokyo

10 9 8 7 6 5 4 3 2 1

Library of Congress Cataloging in Publication Data
Kinard, J. Spencer,
   The worth of a smile.
   Essays delivered by the author on the Mormon Tabernacle Choir's weekly program, Music and the spoken word.
   Includes index.
   1. Church of Jesus Christ of Latter-Day Saints—Sermons. 2. Sermons, American. I. Title.
BX8639.K56W67 252'.09'33 75-42298
ISBN 0-13-969139-1

Foreword

Between the covers of this book will be found a glimpse into the warmth, the personality, the friendliness, and the ability of the author and announcer of "The Spoken Word" —J. Spencer Kinard, who participates so religiously every Sunday morning with the Tabernacle Choir in its regular broadcast which is heard by millions.

In selecting a successor to Elder Richard L. Evans, who performed this service for so many years, it was necessary to find one with the ability to prepare and deliver inspirational messages in conjunction with the performance of the famous Mormon Tabernacle Choir in its weekly program, which has merited the stamp of excellence for its quality both in music and the spoken word. Spence Kinard was that one.

It is fitting that his brief essays should now be available to those who have heard yet wanted to recapture the inspiration of the messages, as well as those who have missed them but would like a book of thoughts to lift their spirits and help them to a better way of life. I commend this book to you, for such is the intent and message of this compilation.

N. Eldon Tanner
1st Counselor, First Presidency
Church of Jesus Christ of
Latter-day Saints

Acknowledgment

The list of people who help contribute to a work that was more than three years in the making is long and always incomplete. But those to whom most of the credit is given are: Paul H. Evans, Executive Producer of "Music and the Spoken Word," who probably had more faith and confidence in me than I have had in myself; Helen Hintze Harlow who worked for Richard L. Evans and had the courage to be my secretary; Arlene Hansen whose enthusiasm for this book led me to do something more than just talk about it; Raymond Haeckel who more than anyone else has been responsible for the judicious editing and contributions; Geniel Robbins who was an aid to Richard Evans for many years and, though retired, graciously agreed to help research each week's effort; Agda Harlow and Wes Bowen for their idea contributions; KSL, Inc., and Bonneville International Corporation for giving me both the time and opportunity; the hundreds of people who have written or requested that this book be published; the dozens of church leaders and teachers who have touched my life and taught me LDS principles from which all my ideas came; my mother who gave me life and led me to the path of eternal life; my father and sisters for their great love; and my wife, Lynette, and children, Holly, David, Jeffrey and Heidi, whose support and inspiration made it all possible.

Thank you all.

Preface

On November 1, 1971, Richard L. Evans, an Apostle of the Church of Jesus Christ of Latter-day Saints (Mormon), died at age 65 in a Salt Lake City hospital of complications of the flu. His unexpected death was a tragic loss to members of the LDS (Mormon) Church. But there was perhaps an even greater loss to the millions of radio and television listeners who knew him as the voice of the Mormon Tabernacle Choir's weekly program, "Music and the Spoken Word." For more than forty-one years, since its beginning in 1929 on nationwide radio, he had been associated with the broadcast, later becoming creator and voice of "The Spoken Word."

In January, 1972, I was called by Gordon B. Hinckley, a member of the Council of Twelve Apostles of the Church, and asked if I would be willing to audition for the "Spoken Word." I did not find that a particularly comforting thought, though one that was most flattering.

A month later, during a telephone conversation, President N. Eldon Tanner (then Second Counselor in the LDS Church First Presidency) told me I had been selected and would begin doing the broadcast the following Sunday. My surprise was so overwhelming that my only response was, "Are you sure you mean *this* coming Sunday?" He was sure.

As LDS people, we believe our leaders are guided and inspired by God in matters concerning the Church. If I believed that—and I did—then I had to believe that they, indeed, the Lord, knew better what course my life should take than I. That for whatever reason, as implausible as it all seemed, I was the one who was to stand, at this time, in the shadow of Richard L. Evans; I was the one who had been asked to serve my Church and God in this way, at this time. I knew in my heart I had no choice but to accept.

On Sunday, February 27, 1972, I stood anxiously dressed in fear before some of the world's finest people and best singers, The Mormon Tabernacle Choir, and was introduced by President Tanner as the "new Spoken Word." With choked voice and tearful eyes, I tried to tell the Choir members there would never be another Richard Evans, but I would do my best to uphold his and their honor and the traditions they had built. This compilation is a partial measure of that effort.

It encompasses a little over three years of weekly writings, organized by subject matter as well as possible. The weekly subjects have never been chosen with any particular book or chapter in mind, but rather have been selected according to the circumstance or, hopefully, inspiration of the moment. While the broadcast is sponsored by the Church of Jesus Christ of Latter-day Saints, I do not think a Christian of any faith would find disagreement with the ideas expressed. In fact, many of the sermonettes deal with non-religious ideas which I hope people of all persuasions will find acceptable. Not all of the writings are included. In some cases, references to lyrics relate to musical selections the Choir performed on the day that message was given. The date on which it originally was broadcast from the Mormon Tabernacle in Salt Lake City is indicated at the end of each sermonette.

It is my hope that this book will bring happiness, guidance or some peace of mind to those who read it, and offer encouragement that may be needed from time to time. I hope it will remind us all from whence comes our happiness and the true *Worth of a Smile*.

J. Spencer Kinard

CONTENTS

1

THE WORTH OF A SMILE

happiness | contentment | joy | satisfaction

emotions | good-byes | tears and maturity

We call it happiness —
a universal goal —
and we seek it in many different ways.

1

The Worth of a Smile

"The face," said Emerson, "reveals what the spirit is doing. It does not lie, but makes a faithful confession to all we meet."[1]

It is probably man's smile which speaks the most universal language—a simple gesture, but one with profound impact on our homes and families, on society at large, and even on our physical well-being. A smile can be sweet and warm, or it can be cold and bitter. At best, it communicates determination, enthusiasm and cheerfulness; it can turn the emotions of despair and defeat upward. It reflects attitude, and can communicate positive feelings to the body for good health. We should share this emotion with others, for it can easily become a habit which will add years to our lives.

Unfortunately, many of us become so involved in our individual affairs, so engrossed in what we are doing, that we are often unaware of our outward appearance. We may feel brotherly love toward others, but perhaps we do not communicate this emotion to them.

Granted, there are troubles and problems facing each of us in the world today, but they are a part of life. It is the selfish man who makes others the victim of his moods. Our responsibility is to make life brighter for others.

What is the worth of a smile? What is its value? How much good can it do? There is a song about little things meaning a lot. Perhaps we do not give enough credit to a simple expression of the face which can bring joy and contentment to both giver and receiver. A smile is the countersign of friendship. It costs nothing, but enriches others. It is of little value until given away.

A smile, to be effective, should come from within. And once initiated, it can spread an unending circle of uplifting influence. A smile only takes a moment, but its memory can last forever.   JULY 9, 1972

Twelve Simple Rules for Happiness

Happiness is a goal we all constantly seek, but there are many differing opinions about how it is achieved. Some believe happiness comes from fame and fortune; others have learned through experience that what they thought would bring the greatest joy actually resulted in sorrow. A philosopher once wisely observed that it is difficult to be happier than other people, "for we believe others to be happier than they are."[2]

Indeed, happiness is not always easy to find because we look for it outside ourselves, when in reality, it comes from within.

There are many formulas for happiness, but today we cite 12 simple rules which, if followed faithfully, will result in sound, secure, joyous living:

1. *First, live a simple life. Be temperate in your habits and avoid selfishness.*

2. *Spend less than you earn. Avoid extravagance and keep out of debt. It may be difficult, but it pays big dividends.*

3. *Think constructively. Train yourself to think clear, accurate, useful thoughts. Avoid unwholesome ideas.*

4. *Try to see the other person's point of view, and resist the tendency to want things your own way.*

5. *Be grateful—glad for the privilege of life and work.*

6. *Rule your moods, don't let them rule you. Remember a lifetime of unhappiness can be caused by a moment of emotional instability.*

7. *Next, give generously. There is no greater joy in life than to bring happiness to others.*

3

8. Be interested in other people.

9. Work with righteous, honest motives. No one who does wrong is ever really happy.

10. Live one day at a time. Concentrate on the immediate task and avoid attempting too much at one time.

11. Develop a hobby or some means of diversion and relaxation.

12. Finally and most important, keep close to God.[3] It will do more to bring happiness than any other single endeavor. And God, in turn, will help keep you close to all other attributes of happiness. It was Christ Himself who, after giving His guideposts for living, said, "If ye know these things, happy are ye if ye do them."[4]

MAY 20, 1973

Imitations of Happiness

Like a sleeping child we all seek escape from the sorrows and difficulties of life. We call it happiness—a universal goal—and we seek it in many different ways. Some of us, unfortunately, follow the wrong roads, but we all search for what we think will bring us happiness.

"[It] has a number of understudies," wrote William George Jordan, "—gratification, satisfaction, contentment, and pleasure—clever imitators that simulate its appearance rather than emulate its method."[5] Pleasure, for example, is only temporary, while happiness may be permanent. But

4

often we grasp one of the imitators instead of the genuine article, because it is easier to obtain. Happiness does not come easily or without effort; it will never be found on life's bargain table.

Paradoxically, happiness is often found hiding in the midst of sorrow, trial and hardship—waiting to rise above all other conditions. It is there for a reason: for without the one we would not know the other. As one prophet stated, "For it must needs be, that there is an opposition in all things...the one being sweet and the other bitter."[6]

Only man can attain real joy. The imitations, the understudies belong to other creatures. And happiness must come from within. It consists not of having, but of being; not of possessing, but of giving. To again quote Jordan, "Man might possess everything tangible in the world and yet not be happy, for happiness is the satisfying of the soul...not the body...A martyr at the stake may have happiness that a king on his throne might envy."[5] Man creates his own happiness through experience, through sharing, giving and, above all, through loving.

"Unhappiness is the hunger to get; happiness is the hunger to give. True happiness must have the tinge of sorrow outlived, the sense of pain softened...[and] the chastening of loss...transmuted...into love and sympathy with others."[5]

As we have said before, happiness can only be found by following the teachings of our Lord and Savior. To seek it outside of the gospel of Jesus Christ is like trying to search the desert for a school of fish.

How grateful we should be for the wisdom and the love that sent the Savior to suffer, bleed and die in order that we might find complete happiness and everlasting life.   OCTOBER 21, 1973

5

The Commandments Are for Our Happiness

"The Lord is my shepherd; I shall not want...."[7] A small girl reportedly once misquoted the first line from the 23rd Psalm this way: "The Lord is my shepherd, that's *all* I want!"

Wouldn't it be wonderful if we could be so firm in our decision as to where we are going, who we are following, what we will do next; if we could say no matter what the difficulty, or whatever the trial or tribulation, we will follow the Savior and keep His commandments.

But too often we choose to compromise. We choose to serve two masters, or three or four. Matthew wrote, "No man can serve...God and mammon."[8] And we need not do so, for the commandments were not given to cause us trouble, but to help us find our way through life.

Surely, at best, life is difficult—it was not intended to be easy. But, just as surely, there came One to show us the best way, a guide who promised us safe passage if we but follow instructions.

"Be not afraid of life..." wrote William James.[9] And the Savior might have added, "—if ye keep my commandments." And what of those commandments? Are they so difficult that there are any of us who cannot keep them? Or, more importantly, are there any of us who would not want to keep them? The commandments are for our own good, our own peace and comfort; for our own happiness. As King David wrote: "Yea, though I walk through the valley of the shadow of death, I will fear no evil: for thou art with me; thy rod and thy staff they comfort me... my cup runneth over."[7]

We need such comfort in our lives, such assurance of where we are going, of what we are going to do. If we are to enjoy the things we ought to enjoy, then we must

6

follow the teachings of the Master; teachings that were given as a means by which we can lighten our load, cast our burdens on the water; teachings given with love and understanding, with gentleness and kindness.

The Lord's commandments are here not to hinder, but to help us. And "If ye know these things, happy are ye if ye do them."[10]   MARCH 5, 1972

Partings...

There are few things in life more emotional than saying good-bye to loved ones. Whether the separation is temporary or for a lifetime, parting is always difficult and often filled with sadness.

The difficulty is that we like to be with those we love, and we find it painful to part with them. The final good-bye is always the most sorrowful. Samuel Butler said, "...I can generally bear the separation, but I don't like the leave-taking."[11]

We usually measure our separation with time and circumstance. Fortunately, many are tempered with new challenges that lie ahead. What parent has not accompanied a young son or daughter to the first day of school with excitement and pleasure at the opportunities therein, but saddened with the realization that it is the beginning of a growing separation between parent and child? The good-byes occur again and again, and then suddenly it is not just another day at the neighborhood school, but a parting for a year at college or employment in another town. We are always grateful for the new challenges but saddened at the partings.

Those mixed emotions are again renewed when children marry or move away, taking precious grandchildren with them. Our sadness comes from wanting to hold

7

close all that is dear. Yet, we find joy and happiness in our relinquishment. Bertrand Russell wrote, "To be without some of the things you want is an indispensable part of happiness."[12]

The degree of our emotional strain at the time of parting is always multiplied by the length and distance of the expected separation. The longer we think our loved ones will be gone, the more difficult the departure. For that reason, no separation is more difficult to endure than death. It seems so permanent. Indeed, the grief is often unbearable for those who believe it does last forever. Yet, it is incomprehensible that God would give us such deep capacity for love and compassion only to have our relationships with one another end at the grave. Gratefully it is not so. The greatest blessing we have is eternal life and the knowledge that all separations need only be temporary. Some are longer than others, but still only temporary when measured in eternities.   SEPTEMBER 1, 1974

Tears of Joy and of Sorrow

The shedding of tears expresses some of life's greatest emotions. It is often like a cleansing of the soul; and, contrary to what many may think, it is a useful and often necessary part of life. There are times when the only immediate relief for pain, frustrations, fear or grief is crying.

Children undoubtedly find much comfort through their freedom to cry when their emotions need it. But many of us—particularly men—feel that to shed tears would be admitting a weakness. Washington Irving thought of it as a strength. "There is a sacredness in tears," he wrote. "They are not the mark of weakness, but of power. They speak more eloquently than ten thousand tongues. They are the messengers of overwhelming grief, of deep contrition, and of unspeakable love."[13]

8

Not all tears are shed in times of fear or difficulty. Tears can and rightfully do flow at the joyful reunion of families, especially following a trying ordeal. Many tears of happiness and love have resulted from a wife's expression of appreciation, a father's moment of understanding, or a child's gift of love. We can be moved to tears by a beautiful song, a lovely poem, an emotional book, or a tender movie or play. Those quiet, joyful tears are an appropriate expression of one's feelings.

But what may affect the emotions of one, may not influence another, as our emotions and crying are deeply personal and private experiences. They are something we can't always control and seldom come at a moment of our own choosing. But still tears are something we need to control as much as possible because of their private and personal nature. There are times when life deals such a crushing blow that all we want to do is sob uncontrollably. Yet, circumstances won't always allow it and so we must wait until we can find ourselves alone in our secret place of prayer. There we can pour out our heart to our Father in heaven letting the tears flow as they may. Crying then, when coupled with prayer, can have a comforting, reassuring effect. It is, in fact, a mark of humility.

Yes, tears, when shed not unwisely or in forceful deceit, are an important and meaningful part of life. They are an honest expression of our emotions.   MARCH 31, 1974

Don't Pull Up the Flowers

Maturity is a completed stage or condition in the growth process, sometimes developing slowly, often painfully. Some arrive at it sooner than others, and some never do. Sometimes we deny ourselves the blessings of maturity, and other times those around us interfere.

9

Perhaps we can learn a lesson about maturity from our own gardens. To plant and water a seed does not automatically produce a mature flower. Continued watering, weeding, pruning, and perhaps, even shelter is required before the plant blossoms into full maturity. But sometimes, like children, we become impatient and pull up the plant to see if the roots have taken hold. Sometimes we do the same with people.

It takes time for deep-seated, mature roots to develop. A friend describes two trees near his home, one growing in the center of a well-groomed lawn, the other along a dry ditch bank near a dusty road. One day a strong wind toppled the olive tree on the lawn, but not the old, mature cottonwood. The olive tree had been watered so well that its roots stayed near the surface and could not resist the force of the wind. But the cottonwood had sunk its tentacles deep in order to drink of the water of life, and it survived the gale. That is part of the maturing process. We must allow our roots to take a firm hold, so the whims and temptations of life will not destroy us.

Now our Father in heaven has carefully placed us in this earthly garden and given us His commandments into which we can sink our roots. But some of us, like the olive tree, have chosen not to establish a strong root system. Instead, we follow the immature path of least resistance and are vulnerable to the winds of adversity. We may be old in years, but we lack maturity and wisdom.

It is also important to understand the process by which others achieve maturity. Many individuals are like the tulip bulb which lies dormant beneath the surface for months awaiting the time to sprout and blossom. If we pull it up to examine its growth, there will be no blossom. The same danger faces people.

Often it is difficult to be patient with loved ones who appear to be standing still. We believe they may be making wrong choices or ignoring wise counsel. But perhaps they are developing roots which will sustain them in the fight for maturity—roots of confidence, security, understanding and patience. If we are too anxious, we may damage the roots before they take hold.

Each of us has his own timetable for growth. But regardless of the length of time required, we must not disturb the root system if we wish to harvest the blessings of maturity.

NOVEMBER 10, 1974

Listening With the Heart

All of our senses are critically needed, but none are more vital to our enjoyment and appreciation of life than the sense of sight and the sense of sound. Nearly all the information we assimilate comes through these two faculties. They are the cornerstones of our learning process.

The changing seasons make us keenly aware of our ability to see and hear. We see autumn leaves changing colors and we hear the wind rustle them to the ground. There are the cheers of football fans, the silence of falling snowflakes, the rare beauty of a frost-covered morning bathed in golden sunlight—these are the sights and sounds of nature's autumn work.

How blessed are those of us who possess these precious gifts of sight and sound. Yet, because we have them, we may miss the more gentle and subtle messages communicated. We refer specifically to another type of hearing which the Lord has blessed us with—the ability to listen with the heart.

It has been said that talk is the activity of the mouth while listening is the activity of the heart. What mother has not responded to the cry of her infant and known of its hunger or pain or anger? And this without words, for she listens and understands through the spirit of love.

11

Meaning is not conveyed in words alone but exists in the human experience. When we listen only to words we usually misunderstand the intended communication. It is only when we listen with the heart that we begin to comprehend, begin to empathize and understand the feelings and ideas being expressed.

André Gide said, "Each of us really understands in others only those feelings he is capable of producing himself."[14] So as we build our own archive of emotional experiences, we will be better equipped to understand others, to really listen to what they are saying. And this, in turn, will increase our own knowledge, sensitivity and understanding, and thereby even further expand our listening ability.

Yes; listening is more than just hearing words or sounds. Whether we are tuned in on nature, or listening to our family and friends, this valuable gift requires thoughtful attention and emotional understanding; for listening with our heart is the only way to really hear the message being transmitted. NOVEMBER 17, 1974

The Well of Happiness

There is reassurance in the lyrics which say, "Let nothing ever grieve thee, distress thee, nor fret thee."[15] We all encounter these anxieties. They are a necessary part of our eternal progress, for without them we would not know joy. The reassurance is in knowing that we can overcome them. It is sad to see someone defeated by distress, someone who has the ability to conquer his troubles, as the song suggests, by "heeding God's good will."[15]

Marcus Aurelius once remarked, "Nothing happens to anybody which he is not fitted by nature to bear."[16]

God has given us the abilities we need to successfully manage our lives, but He has promised us the full use of these personal resources only if we stay close to Him.

Unfortunately there seems to be a feeling among many people that this life should be used for a pleasure hunt. They believe there will be time enough later for religion, that religion isn't necessary now—at least not very much of it. Sometimes the theory seems to work—until difficulties arise, then a general malaise and disillusionment sets in, and soon the frantic search for inner comfort and renewed confidence begins. But there is no strength to be found in material pleasures and treasures: solace can only come from within.

Everyone wants to bypass the anxieties in life, but too often we fail to realize our condition has occurred because we have left God. "Anxiety increases," wrote Fulton J. Sheen, "in direct ratio and proportion as man departs from God."[17]

We all thirst after righteousness, but all of us do not recognize the thirst. Young and old run to and fro drinking from different wells, searching for the water that will feed the soul, but knowing not where to find the well of "everlasting life."

To lose God is to lose our purpose in life. To find Him is to find the thirst-quenching well of happiness.

SEPTEMBER 23, 1973

2

WHERE LIFE MATTERS MOST

---

home | family and marriage

*Our family is the most
important association we have.
Its importance cannot be overstressed.*

Where Life Matters Most

Probably no word known to man strikes a more responsive chord than the word "home." As Charles Angoff said, "Home is where you hang your memories."[1]

And our memories of home are usually pleasant or unpleasant in direct proportion to the amount of love we experience there—love between husband and wife, parent and child, brother and sister. Yes, home and love, or in a word, the family, are the cornerstones of our society.

An effective family creates an environment which provides more than food and shelter. It offers a framework in which members may learn to interact with one another, where they may express ideas and emotions, and learn to give and take and share with one another; for without question, a family is where we learn to experience and express love.

Actually, love is a process of natural growth which develops from within through proper family experiences. It is a gift that we unconsciously reciprocate to those who express their love to us. Most of the emotional strengths we have are built through love at home. Conversely, many of the emotional problems encountered, especially among children, have their origin in family life.

It was a philosopher long ago who said, "Train up a child in the way he should go and when he is old, he will not depart from it."[2] The challenge for that training lies within the walls of our homes. Whether our teaching is intentional or not, whether it is positive or negative, the learning process occurs daily in the home. And parents must realize that they cannot abdicate that responsibility to others.

The honorary chairman of national Family Unity Month, Ernie Ford, has wisely pointed out that the strength of a nation is measured by the strength of its families. "I can think of nothing sweeter in all the world," he said, "than a home where the father is doing his duty within those walls, living an exemplary life, realizing his greatest responsibility is to his family. And with a wife who loves and sustains him in all his righteous endeavors, where the children honor and obey their parents....God grant that we never be too busy to do the things that matter most,..."[3] God grant that we always understand the importance of a family's love at home.   APRIL 20, 1975

The Importance of the Family

The best place to practice and develop the principle of forgiveness is in our homes, as we conduct our daily family affairs.

The family unit is one of the great tools the Creator provided to help keep us on course. It is in a family setting that we most often learn about love, forgiveness, self-discipline and work. It is the best place to acquire beliefs and values. It is there we should learn the lessons of life.

Our family is the most important association we have. Its importance cannot be overstressed. The late spiritual leader David O. McKay offered this wise counsel: "No other success can compensate for failure in the home."[4] And, as Harold B. Lee advised, "The most important work you will ever do...will be within the walls of your own home."[5] If we will work as hard at improving our own families as we do at many of the other things we attempt, our entire world will be a better place in which to live.

Family success does not happen automatically. It is a task which requires high priority and one that we cannot begin too soon. We must pray and work to develop pleasant family relationships, the vital foundation of which is loving parents.

16

Young people would do well to remember that a proper partner and a proper courtship are vital keys to a happy marriage and a successful family. Unhappy family relations is one of the greatest tragedies in life. None of us would willfully choose such an existence, yet, that is what we do when we make hasty or improper choices in building a marriage.

One of the greatest gifts mankind has is freedom. We are free to set our own course; free to raise our own families; free to build our own society. We should remember that "...concentrating on the quality of life in the home is, ultimately, the best way to raise the quality of life in society."[6]

The life that is spent improving the family is a life that is full and rich and beautiful. But too often we are "simple souls who stray" and who find that challenge difficult. Indeed, there can be no more important challenge than the success and happiness of our families.

OCTOBER 8, 1972

Marriage Is...

There is no union under heaven that is more blessed, requires more effort, or is more important than a successful marriage. It has been written that marriage is "the highest happiness on earth...Every man who is happily married is a successful man even if he has failed in everything else."[7]

But marriages are not automatically successful. Like everything else of value, they require work and personal sacrifice. Wilferd Peterson points out that the big things in marriage are really the little things we do everyday:

"It is never being too old to hold hands. It is remembering to say, 'I love you,' at least once a day."[8]

17

Happiness in marriage is not taking your partner for granted. "It is doing things for each other...in the spirit of joy [not out of duty]. It is not looking for perfection in each other, [but] cultivating flexibility, patience, understanding and a sense of humor."[8]

A happy marriage is "having the capacity to forgive and forget. It is finding room for the things of the spirit. It is a common search for the good and the beautiful. [And] it is not only marrying the right partner, [but] *being* the right partner."[8]

A successful life with another person comes through a deep, abiding, unselfish love nurtured over many years. "Contrary to many love stories," wrote one author, "it is not during the first year of bliss that most dangers crop up. Marriages do not, like dropped chinaware, smash as a result of that first quarrel which the newly married hope is unthinkable. Marriage is a rooted thing, a growing and flowering thing that must be tended faithfully. [Without] that mutual effort, we are apt to find some day that our marriage...has been withering imperceptibly."[9]

May we all resolve to renew our marriage vows by remembering these words of Helen Steiner Rice:

"[Marriage] is sharing and caring, giving and forgiving,...laughing together, weeping together, praying together...and thanking God for each other."[10]

Indeed, marriage is a great blessing, but we must not forget to nurture and care for it.   JANUARY 6, 1974

"It Is Not Marriage That Fails..."

Every year throughout the world millions of couples are married—many for the first time. Marriage is an exciting, momentous time in a person's life. One author wrote, "There is something about a wedding-gown prettier than...any other gown in the world."[11] Certainly, there is nothing more highly ordained of the Lord than a proper marriage.

Recently I watched a young bride, seeking the blessings and happiness which marriage can provide, take the hand of her chosen before the altar of God. With tears streaming down her cheeks, she put her arms around loved ones and said, "I've never been happier." If the marriage is a good one, the happiness felt by the bride and groom that day will be magnified many times through the years. But contrast that rewarding moment with a hastily arranged dash to a Justice of the Peace, where the atmosphere may be cold and void of spirituality. "Hasty marriage seldom proveth well," said Shakespeare.[12]

People get married for a variety of reasons—many times for the wrong ones. But something we all need to remember, as one of our nation's spiritual leaders once said, is that "Marriage is an enterprise for adults."[13] One of the great tragedies this country will face during the coming year is the nearly one million marriages that are expected to end in divorce. That means broken homes, broken hearts and, many times, broken lives.

Marriage is important. It is basic to our way of life, and it is ordained of God. But there is more to it—much more—than just a wedding ceremony. Marriage means joy and heartache...sharing and planning...love and mutual trust. It builds and tests our character, as Harry Emerson Fosdick pointed out when he said, "It is not marriage that fails; it is people that fail. All that marriage does is show people up."[14]

So, yes, young people, and those young at heart—get married. But set sail on this fulfilling journey for the right reason, at the right time and from the proper port. And when you do, remember—as we all have need to remember—to build that marriage with LOVE; for in the words of the song, "Our God is a God of love,...Bless'd is the family where love abides....[and] Bless'd are the children whose fondest memories,...are of such love."[15]

JANUARY 14, 1973

A Kind, Thoughtful Word

Recently a friend of mine lost his father, suddenly and without warning. My friend's sorrow was not only at his father's passing, but also because it had been a long time since he had told his father how much he thought of him.

When was the last time you told someone close to you, "I love you," or "I'm grateful for all you do"?

We all need to be encouraged, appreciated, rewarded in life; and one of the most simple and pleasing rewards we can give or receive is a kind, thoughtful word.

Think back to the last time someone came up to you and, without particular reason, told you how much he admired you, or appreciated what you did, or merely offered a simple and sincere compliment. Remember how it brightened your whole day?

Too often, perhaps, we feel we need special occasions to say special things. We only tell Mother we love her on Mother's Day, Father is a great guy only on Father's Day and his birthday, students are congratulated only when they are good; yet, they need love most when they are not so good.

To be wanted, to be loved, to be appreciated is a basic human need; but the times we tell people they are wanted, loved, and appreciated are too few and far between.

My friend's father had just been out on a "date" with his "bride" of many years. They had been to dinner and were driving home. He had barely told his wife how much he loved her and how grateful he was for their life together when he, unexpectedly, collapsed in her lap and died. Surely that dear wife is grateful today that her hus-

20

band took a moment to express his feelings, and didn't wait for a special occasion to do so.

That does not mean that we should ignore special occasions. Mother likes to be told she is loved and appreciated on Mother's Day also—in fact, would be disappointed if she wasn't. But, to do the usual, the expected, is easy. To do the unusual, the unexpected, requires special thought; but the happy result is a meaningful and lasting remembrance.

MAY 14, 1972

"There's No Place Like Home"

"Home, home, sweet, sweet home/ Be it ever so humble, there's no place like home."[16] For most of us, no matter who we are or where we go in life, there is always a particular place in some corner of the world we can call our own. And there is no better way to appreciate this spot than to be away from it. Those who spend much of their time traveling are the first to admit that the best part of any trip is the return home.

We are now approaching the end of the vacation season in this country and although the sights and experiences may have been rejuvenating, there is still an inner sense of relief that comes in finally returning to the place we call home. It doesn't seem to matter whether we've stayed in luxurious hotels or camped on a mountain trail, home is still the most cherished place of all, and there are few who return who don't happily sigh, "It's great to be home!"

Revisit sometime a house you once lived in. You will find that your feelings about it are not the same. Many fond memories may be rekindled, but your former home and fortress seems like a mere shell. The feeling of belonging—the comfort and security you once knew are gone.

21

What makes a home so special? Among other things it provides a focal point for us in life, a starting place for all we do and a retreat to soothe our fatigue and wounds. But the most important ingredient in a home is love. Anyone can build a house, but it takes love to build a home. Many have left their homes—young and old alike—because they felt there was no love for them there, and without love all the pleasures of a home are meaningless. We must not make the mistake of providing only the material house. We must fill it with love.

Dr. John Henry Jowett once described a home as a place of affection, of fervent hope and genial trust. He said, "The New Testament does not say very much about homes; it says a great deal about things that make them. It speaks of life and love and joy and peace and rest. If we get a house and put these into it, we shall have secured a home."[17]

In the song "Home, Sweet Home" John Payne reminds us, "'Mid pleasures and palaces though we may roam,/Be it ever so humble, there's no place like home."[16]

SEPTEMBER 3, 1972

3

THE INNOCENCE OF CHILDREN

children | parenthood | family love

*If the foundation of a well-ordered society
is a healthy, happy home,
then the problem of lawlessness will not
be solved by more laws or legislation;
but by fathers and mothers
exerting a moral influence and
example in their own families,
tempered with love and understanding.*

The Innocence of Children

Little in the world is as awe-inspiring as the birth of a child. To see such a tiny creation function as it does—instilled with the spirit and soul of an individual—should be testimony enough for any man that God lives.

As children grow and we witness the beauty and innocence of their character, we have further understanding of the Lord's statement that "of such is the kingdom of heaven."[1] Who else can love without needing reasons why, or offer help without expecting something in return? Yes, some of life's greatest joys are discovered through children.

What is a boy? Or what is a girl? A few lines from the writings of Alan Beck point out some of the delightful pleasures of children:

> *A boy is Truth with dirt on its face, Beauty with a cut on its finger, Wisdom with bubble gum in its hair, and the Hope of the future with a frog in its pocket...[And] when you come home at night with only the shattered pieces of your hopes and dreams, he can mend them like new with two magic words, "Hi Dad!"*

> *A girl is Innocence playing in the mud, Beauty standing on its head, and Motherhood dragging a doll by the foot....But when your dreams tumble down and the world is a mess...she can make you a king [or queen] when she climbs on your knee and whispers, "I love you best of all"*[2]

Indeed, children are the light of the world. They are a continual reminder of many important attributes we should all strive to develop. The Savior told us, "Except... [we] become as little children, [we] shall not enter into the kingdom of heaven."[3] If only we could remember that counsel. The poet put it this way:.

24

Last night my little boy confessed to me
Some childish wrong;
And kneeling at my knee,
He prayed with tears —
"Dear God, make me a man
Like Daddy — wise and strong;
I know you can."

Then while he slept
I knelt beside his bed,
Confessed my sins,
And prayed with low-bowed head —
"O God, make me a child
Like my child here —
Pure, guileless,
Trusting Thee with faith sincere."[4]

But children grow up, and the innocence which was once ours and now is theirs will soon be left for still another generation. And so the challenge: to live our lives with some portion of that child-like innocence that we may always be teachable and may some day inherit a place in our Father's kingdom.   OCTOBER 7, 1973

Songs Our Mothers Taught Us

Many of us have wept in gratitude in recalling the songs our mothers taught us. Indeed, nothing seems to stir the soul more than the pleasant memory of familiar melodies, and no song in the world rings with greater tenderness and affection than one sung by a mother to her child.

Of all the miracles in the world, motherhood is one of the most common, and still one of the most treasured. The love a mother feels for her child is a natural instinct given by God, and only a willing heart is required to keep it.

25

Little is more beautiful or more indicative of such love than the serene sight of a mother cradling her child. As a friend once said, "Any mother appears hallowed and strikingly beautiful when she has a babe in her arms."[5] Were it not so, the world's authors and artists would not have written so many verses, painted so many pictures, or sculptured so many statues of mother and child.

"...The most important, the most honorable and desirable task which can be set by any woman," wrote Theodore Roosevelt, "is to be a good and wise mother...."[6] And it is not only the sense of duty that makes mothers accept this challenging assignment—they welcome the responsibility because of the inner yearning God has given them to love children as only a mother can. And one of the most cherished of all child-rearing moments comes when a mother holds a babe in her arms and sings it a lullaby. It matters not that the child may miss the meaning of the words or the rhythm of the tune. Nor does it matter how well the mother sings. What does matter is the message of love which a mother communicates.

The miracle of it all is that every babe can feel the strength, security and love that comes when a mother sings a lullaby.

MAY 13, 1973

"...Of Such Is the Kingdom of Heaven"

Little in this world is sweeter, more peaceful or innocent than a sleeping child. As one writer put it, "I do not know of a better shrine before which a father or mother may kneel or stand...I do not know of a holier place, a temple where one is more likely to come into closer touch with all that is infinitely good, where one may come nearer to seeing and feeling God...[than at the side of a sleeping child]."[7]

Former U.S. President Herbert Hoover also remarked that "Children are the most wholesome part of the race...for they are freshest from the hand of God."[8] And it was the Master Himself who said, "...for of such is the kingdom of heaven."[9]

As adults we must help our children maintain much of their heavenly innocence. We have a responsibility, not to shelter them, but to help them understand—as one young man said—that "it isn't the length of our days that we live, but it is the quality of life that becomes most valuable and meaningful to us."[10] We need to teach our children sound principles which will help them realize a serene and meaningful life.

A set of guidelines to assist us with our youth has been prepared by an unknown author. They include the following points: First and foremost, teach them principles of brotherly love, and of God. Give them our attention, for one day it will be too late. Give them a sense of value, a sense of courage and conviction; of self-reliance, respect of others. Help them develop a sense of humor, an understanding of discipline and the will to work. Help them discover the satisfaction of sharing and a love of justice and truth. Then give them the most precious gift of all—the knowledge that they are loved, not only by earthly parents, but by a literal Father in heaven as well.

If we will meet, in some measure, these responsibilities to our children, then the end of each day will find us able, as an Old Welsh poem states, to sleep with peace "all through the night."   FEBRUARY 25, 1973

27

The Majesty of a Mother's Love

It is doubtful that any of us truly appreciate all our mothers have done for us. It is mother who nurtures us, cares for us and guides us. She is our first and most important teacher, for her lessons have the most impact on our lives. We make our first fumbling attempts at speech through our mother's promptings, and from her learn many other basic skills. And most important, it is a mother's example that shapes our character. As Henry Beecher wisely observed, "The mother's heart is the child's schoolroom."[11] Little wonder that Lincoln owned, "All that I am or hope to be, I owe to my angel mother."[12]

Yes, it is a mother's love, patience and example that supports and influences us while we learn life's most important lessons, that helps us develop our ideals and guiding principles. No one can teach those lessons as forcefully or as well as she, especially in those first few, all-important years of a child's life. Indeed, more often than not, as Walter Landor expressed it, "Children are what [their] mothers are;..."[13]

It is no accident and should be no surprise that most crime and other destructive behavior comes from those who come from broken homes. Mothers who do not accept or who refuse to accept the importance of their calling are destined to pay the price of sorrow or disappointment in later years. Ironically, there are many young mothers who search for careers outside the home rather than fulfill the supremely creative role of shaping the character and lives of their children. "When you educate a man," wrote Dr. McIver, "you educate an individual; when you educate a woman you educate a whole family."[14]

Yes, motherhood is an enriching experience.

Hopefully, we can all reflect on our childhood and more fully understand and appreciate the overwhelming contributions our mothers have made to our lives.   MAY 11, 1975

Realistic Parenthood

"Nobody knows [the] trouble I've seen...Glory Hallelujah."[15] Indeed, there is much truth in those words, and although we are never fully aware of another's burdens, we would probably not be willing to trade our own for someone else's.

One way to eliminate or reduce the often overpowering feeling of becoming submerged in our own problems is not to overlook or underestimate the many successes we have experienced in life. Often we are so involved in trying to reach the top—whatever or wherever the top may be—that we fail to see the good we have accomplished along the way. We are inclined to multiply our problems and become so overwhelmed with what we are unable to achieve, that our victories seem insignificant, and quickly fade into the past.

It is a fact that one person's weakness is another person's success, and no one can be successful in all things. Our families are a good example of this phenomenon. Often parents try to be all things, at all times, to their children, and frustration rushes in when they realize their goal is beyond reach.

One father may understand and relate to his ten-year-old son but have great difficulty with his five-year-old child. That does not mean he is a failure as a father, only that he has greater ability in dealing with one age group than another. One father may find it easy to read a story to his child, while another is more comfortable playing a game. But neither one is a poor parent because he has limitations. In the eyes of children, the worth of a father is measured in terms of love, not in degree of ability.

A nationally syndicated columnist, Sydney Harris, once wrote, "It is important...for parents to understand and accept their own limitations...just as they must accept the child's limitations of temperament and talent. Otherwise, [parents] will feel guilty and blame themselves for inadequacies that are not their fault."[16]

All fathers can't be great fishermen, or auto mechanics, or singers, or champion ballplayers. But more important, no one expects them to be. The point to remember is that every father—every parent—has certain abilities which can bring family success, abilities which can be multiplied with love, patience and understanding.

We must accent the positive, for small victories along the way will renew our self-esteem and make many of life's seemingly formidable problems disappear.

JUNE 17, 1973

No Greater Gift

It has been said that the breakdown of the home and family is probably the single greatest cause of lawlessness and disorder in the world today. Sociologists tell us that the majority of those in prisons and penal institutions come from broken homes. If this is true—if the foundation of a well-ordered society is a healthy, happy home, then the problems will not be solved by more laws or legislation; but by fathers and mothers exerting a moral influence and example in their own families, tempered with love and understanding.

If every young man was properly trained by his father and taught the lessons of honesty, obedience and justice, then theft and murder could become a rare occurrence. If mothers taught their daughters moral cleanliness by example, much of the sorrow young women encounter in life would disappear. And if families developed a true love and concern for one another, perhaps we could eliminate much of the growing drug problem, which often stems from the search for identity.

A friend of mine who works with juvenile offenders said there is one characteristic common to most young people who are in trouble. They feel that no one loves them, that no one cares. And they are most heartbroken, because they feel their own family is unconcerned.

Our children need to know that we love them. Perhaps the next time we consider a gift for our children we should consider a gift of our personal time. An hour between father and son or mother and daughter can bring more joy than any material item, and it will have far greater impact than our just telling them we love them.

What is the perfect family? William Aikman said it is "...where enlightened Christianity prevails; where woman is exalted to her true and lofty place...where husband and wife are one in honor, influence and affection, and where children are a common bond of care and love."[17]

If society is to be well-ordered, well-instructed and well-governed, then we must teach and practice similar principles in the home. Children need the love of parents and of each other, and parents need the love of children. There can be no greater gift than this.   JUNE 18, 1972

"How Well Have We Done?"

The lyrics from the musical *Fiddler on the Roof* poignantly portray the thoughts of parents as they watch the marriage of their children. That same scene is repeated daily as children mature and leave home, and parents reflect on the hours spent with their children—hours which have passed so quickly.

The fall season, in particular, is a time for such thoughts, as students leave for school, many to be away from home for the first time. Parents can not help but wonder, "How well have we done?" There is no sure answer, there are no guarantees, but there are some things that can be done to tilt the scales in favor of success. To parents and future parents we offer these suggestions from two doctors who have spent their lives keeping children healthy:[18] Parents should always regard their children as gifts from the Lord, for we have been told that "of such is the kingdom of heaven."[19] They should not try to force their children into some idealistic mold or image, for everyone has a right to be an individual. However, as children seek that individuality they may often fail. That is when they need encouragement most.

Children also need discipline, but they need it with love. As the Lord made known to one of His prophets, "[Reprove at times] with sharpness...then showing forth afterwards an increase of love toward him whom thou has reproved..."[20]

Another suggestion from these doctors is for parents to be united in their approach to life. If conflicts arise, particularly on points of discipline, they should be discussed in private, not in the presence of the children.

One fault most parents seem to have is spoiling their children, and this fault becomes serious when parents attempt to substitute material things for love.

Perhaps the most important advice the doctors give is for parents to remember that children learn best from example. As parents, we must live the way we want our children to become, for we are the most influential examples in their lives.   SEPTEMBER 2, 1973

32

4

PEACE BEGINS WITH EACH OF US

peace | brotherhood | society | service

neighbors | giving | love | passion

forgiveness and prejudice

Life was not intended
to be lived alone,
and our relationship with our fellowman
is an integral part of our relationship with ourselves.

33

Peace Begins With Each of Us

The peace which follows a war—any war in any country—is always fragile and difficult to maintain because the bitterness created is deep and takes time to fade away. But it will disappear if we replace it with love.

There is a difference between peace and love. Peace is to stop firing weapons, but love is to have no need for them; peace comes after a war, love is what prevents one. Peace is temporary and part of man's mortal goal; but love makes peace permanent, and belongs to God's eternal plan.

The need for peace and love goes far beyond the boundaries of nations or the personalities of presidents and diplomats. It begins with each of us. There is a proverb which says, "If there is righteousness in the heart, there is beauty in the character; if there is beauty in the character, there is love in the home; if there is love in the home, there is harmony in the nation; and if there is harmony in the nation, there is peace in the world."[1]

The differences between peace and love also apply at home. People at peace speak to each other, those in love communicate. Peace is forgetting a grievance; love means true forgiveness. People can exist in peace, but they live together through love. Peace often comes late and leaves early, while love enters quietly and lasts forever. Peace is the end—love is the beginning.

And so, as caretakers of this world, we have a continuing opportunity to turn peace into love. We, who have conquered disease, transplanted organs, built every kind of machine conceivable and hurled men into space, still face the greatest challenge of all—to spread love and lasting peace throughout the world. And the beginning of this great responsibility is not in the capitals of the world, but in each human heart—in the conduct of our individual lives.

JANUARY 28, 1973

Brotherhood—Then Peace

Much has been said and written—especially by the young —about peace in the world, but as one author wrote, "You may call for peace as loudly as you wish, but where there is no brotherhood there can in the end be no peace."[2]

We all have need to improve our relationships with one another. We all have need to be more aware of the urgent need for brotherhood.

It is unfortunate that that which becomes commonplace in life, often tends to become unimportant. Many of the problems of today's society have been with us for a long time, and because they have, we tend to become less concerned about them than perhaps we ought to.

Today we give little more than a passing thought to men circling the earth and traveling to the moon. Yet contrast this to the early days of space travel when all the world seemed to take notice. In 1970 three Americans on the Apollo 13 flight were making an emergency return trip to earth because of an explosion in their spacecraft. For several days, the world united in a brotherly concern for those three astronauts. Like Aristotle said, "A common danger unites even the bitterest enemies."[3]

Why can't we have the same unity, the same sense of urgency in expressing brotherhood in our lives, at times when life is not so dramatic but when the results are just as important? There is a need for brotherhood all over the world and we cannot and should not ignore it.

"It's easy enough to be friendly to one's friends," said Gandhi. "But to befriend the one who regards himself as your enemy is the quintessence of true religion."[4]

There are those with whom we disagree, and those who disagree with us, but those differences do not mean there cannot be brotherhood among us. Of all we have in life, a universal brotherhood of man is probably our most precious possession, yet also the one we seem to guard the least.

"You may call for peace as loudly as you wish, but where there is no brotherhood there can in the end be no peace."[2]

APRIL 23, 1972

Our Need to Be Needed

Our needs in life are many and varied, not the least of which is prayer to God. We say to the Lord, "Hear our prayer," not because *He* is in need but because *we* are. And so it is when we sometimes help others, for among our many needs is the need to be wanted and needed.

It is sometimes difficult to satisfy this need in our complex society, because as society has changed throughout the ages, so has the means of service. But the need to serve and give of ourselves has always remained.

We are more richly rewarded when we help others on a one-to-one basis. Modern living requires us to be dependent on others for most of what we have. But that dependence is usually on people we never see—quite a contrast to earlier eras when neighbors helped neighbors build their homes, till their soil and weave their fabric.

The fact that our society is specialized and complex need not take from us the opportunity to enrich ourselves by serving others and being served by them. There is no faster way to get closer to a person than to be asked to do something for him. In a way we are being told we have a needed ability, a talent that is valuable.

Most of our deep and lasting friendships are built upon our willingness to help someone in a moment of need—out of our need for each other. We truly appreciate an individual when we are able to do something for him.

Our involvement with others and the opportunity

36

to serve them brings happiness. And it is most keenly felt when it is a person-to-person involvement through church service, volunteer work or simple neighborliness.

Yes, we need each other. But more than that, we need to be needed. Not so much because others need our help, but because we need the self-esteem and satisfaction of knowing that we served our fellowmen.

Fortunately, life was not intended to be lived alone, and our relationship with our fellowman is an integral part of our relationship with ourselves. OCTOBER 6, 1974

The Gift of Oneself

The words of Brahms' *Requiem* remind us that sorrow comes to all of us for one reason or another, and one of life's most sorrowful moments is when we believe we are not loved.

It is difficult to define love and even more difficult to understand it. But one point is certain: everyone needs love. And it touches not only those who receive it, but those who give it as well. As the French playwright Jean Anouilh said, "Love is, above all, the gift of oneself."[5]

Recently, we spoke of the importance of love in the home, that personal parent-and-child, husband-and-wife kind of love we all treasure. But love in family relationships is not enough. We must care for one another with a love which transcends the boundaries of countries and nationalities. It is a difficult task, but one well worth the effort.

Our world is composed of various customs and cultures. Each of us is rightfully proud of our own heritage, but in the twentieth-century world, transportation and communication have brought the inhabitants of the earth shoulder to shoulder. Nations are no longer isolated; the

37

world has become its own cosmopolitan community—a blend of world neighbors requiring greater love and understanding of one another than ever before.

As the German poet Rainer Maria Rilke wrote, "For one human being to love another...is perhaps the most difficult of all tasks, the ultimate, the last test and proof, the work for which all other is but preparation."[6]

Indeed, all that we do in life could be wasted unless we develop within our hearts a sincere reverence for life and the capacity to love mankind. We must do more than simply love those who love us. That is comparatively easy. The challenge, as our Lord and Savior pointed out, is to "Love [our] enemies, bless them that curse [us], do good to them that hate [us], and pray for them which despitefully use...and persecute [us]."[7]

One of life's greatest lessons and sacrifices is to give of ourselves—to give our love to one another.

AUGUST 26, 1973 from Olympic Sport Hall, Munich, Germany

Unconditional Family Love

We have often spoken of the importance of the family, and of the joy and pleasures that children bring. But that joy and happiness, for both parents and children, must be earned—with love.

Just as the family unit is the basis of our society, so is love the basis of the family. Children need to love their parents, and parents need to love their children. It is a two-way communication, and it is not enough simply to love someone in our hearts. The affection must also be shown and shared.

There are altogether too many young people throughout the world who are convinced that their parents do not love them. They are almost always wrong, but so

38

often parents disguise their love, hiding it behind authority, work or self-interest.

There is no substitute for parental love. Pediatricians say that a baby given love and affection, even in a modest home, is far more likely to become a strong, confident, and responsible adult, than a child raised with an abundance of wealth but without love.

Love is shown in many ways. It is more than just providing physical needs, or a pat on the head or a goodnight kiss. It consists of doing things for and with one another, and the giving of ourselves. Infants need to be held and caressed, youngsters need guidance in school and play, and teenagers need recognition and understanding. Yes, it takes more than just saying so to show someone we love them. It has been said that if families would spend just one night a week together in the home, the majority of family problems would disappear.

Love for one another should be unconditional. And children probably need our love most when they seem least to deserve it—during times of strife and difficulty. As Victor Hugo wrote, "The supreme happiness of life is the conviction of being loved for yourself, or, more correctly, being loved in spite of yourself."[8]

Indeed, children need our unconditional love, in spite of themselves—just as we need their unconditional love.   AUGUST 19, 1973

Honest Praise

No matter who we are or what we do, we all need to be recognized for our achievements in life. But praise presents an interesting paradox, for too much can create vanity and conceit; too little destroys confidence and self-esteem.

"We are all excited by the love of praise,"[9] said Cicero. But Samuel Johnson warned, "Praise, like gold and diamonds, owes its value to its scarcity."[10] Yes, there is a delicate balance, and parents, especially, should give thoughtful consideration to how they apply the principles of praise in the home.

Nothing is more disheartening to a child than to spend hours on a project only to have it ignored, or have it receive perfunctory notice. When we fail to give proper acknowledgment to a child for the good he does, the youngster often resorts to undesirable acts in order to satisfy his craving for recognition, even though he knows he will be punished for his behavior.

We all seek recognition. It is a natural instinct not sought by youth alone. The craving for personal notice sometimes becomes so intense that even adults find themselves making critical errors in judgment in order to attract even the smallest amount of attention.

Perhaps the key to praise is that it must be earned to be of value. It is true that part of the satisfaction we get in life comes in having our work known and appreciated by others. And most of the honest pride we feel comes from the positive recognition given us by our peers. But as one author wrote, "Praise shames me, for I secretly beg for it."[11] And so perhaps do we all, but the shame comes when our inner desire becomes an outer appeal—when we begin asking for recognition through our words and actions. Even though praise may be warranted, it is not a check to be cashed at our demand. It is only of value when it is given voluntarily.

Briefly then, our goal is two-fold: First, to give praise when praise is due, even for the simplest accomplishments. We must not make those around us fight for every word of encouragement. Secondly, we should not seek praise, but let it come from whence it will.

FEBRUARY 3, 1974

The Beginning of Wisdom

A philosopher once suggested that "nothing great in the world has been accomplished without passions,"[12] while yet another warned that "when...passions become masters, they are vices."[13] Indeed, as Emerson observed, "Passion, ...is a powerful spring."[14]

Some years ago a story was written about a fictional place called "Shangri-La." One of the doctrines of *Lost Horizon* was that wisdom begins when our passions are exhausted—an interesting thought which contains some truth, for certainly passion can interfere with good judgment.

What misery, for example, has resulted from the passions for power. It is not a weakness reserved only for high office, but one that can engulf us all. The desire to rule over others infects almost every kind of human relationship.

There is also the passion for possession, which may well be the sickness of our time. Someone said there was a time when we loved people and used things. Now, too often, we love things and use people.

And then there is the passion for self-indulgence. "I've got to do my own thing," we sometimes hear people say, but often it is only a mask for irresponsible behavior, behavior which does not consider the hurt it may bring others, and ignores the fact that "no man is an island."[15]

But simply because uncontrolled passion may bring misery is not sufficient reason to eliminate it as in Shangri-La. For even though passion—like fire—is dangerous, it is still of great value.

What sort of world would we live in without the passion for freedom which has burned in the souls of men? Or what would life be like without the passion for truth and honesty? Nor would we want a world in which there is no passion for justice.

And what of the passion for beauty? Would there be a Handel's *Messiah* or a Michelangelo's *David* without passion?

The answer is obvious: It is not the exhaustion, but the channeling of passion which brings wisdom. Controlled passion enlarges and enriches the human spirit.

There are passions which produce dignity and character, and there are those which make us less than we want to be. It would be well for us to understand the difference, for that basic knowledge may well be the beginning of wisdom.   JANUARY 19, 1975

"Forgive, and Ye Shall Be Forgiven..."

"To err is human," wrote Alexander Pope, "to forgive divine."[16]

We all make mistakes. This is part of our mortal existence, and perhaps that is why there is in each of us a need to be forgiving. We need forgiveness, not only from the Master, but from each other.

Imagine what life would be like if there were no forgiveness? As one philosopher suggests, "The vengeance of long ago would become the torment of today. ..."[17] But fortunately it is not that way. The Lord is willing to forgive. Therefore, should we not be willing to forgive others—even seventy times seven? Remember the words of the Savior, "Forgive, and ye shall be forgiven:..."[18]

One of the greatest difficulties is to forgive those close to us. It has been said that "It is easier to forgive an enemy than to forgive a friend."[19] But the Lord has said that such an oversight can be a greater sin than the one committed against us: "Wherefore, I say unto you, that ye ought to forgive one another; for he that forgiveth

42

not his brother his trespasses standeth condemned before the Lord; for there remaineth in him the greater sin."[20]

Another facet of forgiveness—which involves a degree of inner strength and security—is the ability to not be offended, or take offense. There are far too many who have left their church, their job, their families; who have lost their friends, or committed crimes simply because they have taken offense and were unwilling to forgive.

Forgiveness of others is not something of minor consequence. There can be no greater form of Christianity or humanity. For, as we were promised in the Sermon on the Mount: "...blessed is he, whosoever shall not be offended..."[21]

OCTOBER 1, 1972

Along Life's Highway

One of the traits so perfectly exemplified in the life of our Savior was forgiveness.

In some respects our journey through life can be compared to driving an automobile. Occasionally drivers make a mistake in judgment or become careless in driving habits, and accidents result. So it is as we meet and pass others along life's highway, we occasionally make an unintentional error in judgment which results in an emotional injury. These accidents, as with a car, may be minor or serious. In some cases they may even leave a permanent scar if proper treatment is not given. As medicine helps heal physical injuries, so admitting mistakes and seeking forgiveness aids in correcting emotional injuries.

Since we all make mistakes, we all have need to be forgiven. And more important, we must also be able to forgive the mistakes of others. The ability to forgive is an essential attribute in human relationships, and like most human experiences, it is an act which must be shared to be meaningful. As Shakespeare said of mercy, "It blesseth him that gives, and him that takes."[22] So forgiveness also is a two-sided proposition—we must both forgive and be forgiven.

Forgiveness does not erase the error, but it does make it possible to share the consequences. It allows the forgiver to lighten the burden of the forgiven by sharing the experience. And it requires more than simple words. It is, as Dorothy Sayers suggests, "a re-establishment of a right relationship in which the parties can genuinely feel and behave as freely with one another as though the unhappy incident had never taken place."[23]

Receiving forgiveness also demands an active, conscious effort. It means honest regret and the restoration, as much as possible, of what may have been destroyed. It means feeling right toward the one who has suffered from our action.

Yes, "To err *is* human, to forgive, [*is*] divine."[24] And may we who travel this often bumpy road of life continue to remind ourselves, and teach the "new drivers" that forgiveness—both its bestowal and its receiving—is essential if we are to enjoy a smoother journey.   MAY 4, 1975

"Weeding Out Prejudice"

The gift of liberty is a God-given gift to all men. It stands, as Paul Thompson wrote,

> ...*in majesty in wisdom and virility;*
> *In honor, in trust and righteousness,*
> *And clothed in robes of brotherhood,*
> *It faces heavenward...from whence it came!*[25]

But even then, liberty and freedom are not gifts all men enjoy; not because God would have it that way, but because of the weaknesses of men.

One's right of free agency is deprived, to a greater or lesser degree, by the prejudices of others. Dictators impose their will on entire nations; despots permit only one point of view. But the battle for freedom is not always fought with guns or with laws in the halls of governments. The battle is often waged within the hearts and souls of men, when we, as individuals, impose our biases upon the lives of others. In so doing, we chip away at the foundations of freedom.

To be partial is natural and understandable. The late Edward R. Murrow once said, "Everyone is a prisoner of his own experiences. No one can eliminate prejudices— just recognize them."[26] And recognizing them is usually the most difficult part.

The challenge we face is to prevent our own nearsightedness from restricting the vision of others. No freedom-loving individual would willfully allow his biases to interfere with the rights of others. Yet it happens—it happens because each of us thinks what he is doing is right. When this country was struggling for its independence 200 years ago, one political philosopher observed, "No man is prejudiced in favor of a thing knowing it to be wrong. He is attached to it on the belief of its being right."[27] Obviously, we need not accept every idea and opinion we hear, but we must be willing to listen to others with understanding, for they, too, believe they are right. Our views may differ, but in each case, the strength of conviction comes from the heart, and so should our understanding.

Now there is also an important caution. In eliminating our prejudice, we should not cast aside our personal standards. Jonathan Swift wisely pointed out that "Some men, under the notion of weeding out prejudices, eradicate virtue, honesty and religion."[28]

Yes, world peace begins with peace in each heart. It comes from strong convictions and a willingness to allow others their points of view. That is the peace that produces lasting freedom, the peace that will crown this land with "brotherhood from sea to shining sea." SEPTEMBER 15, 1974

5

THE MEMORIES OF FRIENDSHIP

friends | memories | neighbors and people

*Good friendships add to
the sweetness of life,
and every life needs
the solid foundation which good friendships bring.
But we must also remember
they do not come without effort.*

The Memories of Friendship

Our memories are indelible reminders of the past. They comfort and enrich us with fond recollections of the people, places and events we have known. But of all our memories, none is more precious than that of the friendships we have made.

We recall a song dedicated to a man (David O. McKay) who touched the lives of thousands. He was a friend to many whom he never knew, yet in whose memory he remains a stabilizing influence:

> *He left to other men the path*
> *To wealth, that turns to clay:*
>
> *He left to others hate and wrath*
> *And sought the gentle way.*

The point we would make is that true friends are what make life memorable.

We all like to return to places which have given us fond memories, but upon returning we frequently find that things are not the same because the people associated with the memories are no longer there. To return to an old neighborhood can be a disappointment if all the old neighbors are gone or if there is no one with us to share our memories. We soon learn that it was the people, not the place, that held our affection and interest; that life's most meaningful moments are shared by others. As Antoine de Saint-Exupéry wrote, "Nothing can match the treasure of common memories, of trials endured together, of quarrels and reconciliations and generous emotions."[2]

Indeed, the friendships we build in life, especially those "friendships" with our loved ones, are some of the most enduring treasures we have. The memories of friendship encompass all that we were and all that we are, at all times and in all circumstances.

Part of the challenge we face in cultivating and building true friendships is the ability to make our friends feel they have our love and confidence at all times.

"Oh, the comfort, the inexpressible comfort," wrote one author, "of feeling safe with a person, having neither to weigh thoughts, nor measure words—but pouring them all right out—just as they are—chaff and grain together—certain that a faithful hand will take and sift them—keep what is worth keeping—and with the breath of kindness blow the rest away."[3]   MARCH 17, 1974

The Price of Friendship

It is important in life to have faithful friends on whom we can rely as we travel each day through our increasingly complex world, for friends are an extension of ourselves. They are like a mirror which reflects our successes and helps absorb our errors, and are often the difference between a life full of meaning and a life of loneliness.

Unfortunately, we sometimes confuse "acquaintanceship" with "friendship." In our daily activities we may exude an air of friendship, but many of those relationships are simply superficial acquaintanceships, so superficial, in fact, that we may often feel uncomfortable and try to avoid situations where we must reveal ourselves to those around us. Instead of sharing our ideas and judgments, our opinions and emotions, we censor our inner feelings before we speak. And yet it is those inner feelings —those personal thoughts—which make each of us unique and which are the basis of strong friendships.

The key to developing meaningful relationships is to be honest and open with one another in a spirit of love. We must assure our friends by word and action that we are pleased to advise but intend no criticism, that we can fully respect their efforts and can easily forgive their

48

errors, that we will gladly assist and courageously defend them. Only when we convey that trust will a friend be able to risk coming from behind his emotional shelter to engage in confidential communication.

Friendship is the capacity to feel *with* another person, not *for* him. As Alfred Adler points out, "We learn in friendship to look with the eyes of another person, to listen with his ears and to feel with his heart..."[4]

Good friendships add to the sweetness of life, and every life needs the solid foundation which good friendships bring. But we must also remember they do not come without effort. As Emerson observed, "The only way to have a friend is to be one."[5] APRIL 13, 1975

"Give What You Have..."

We have said before that none of us will pass through this life without affecting the lives of others, for no man exists entirely unto himself.

To some degree, we all depend upon one another. In fact, much of our own happiness is dependent upon others and comes from those around us. But, interestingly, happiness is a result of what we give to our fellowmen— not what we take. The most capable individual always seems to be the one most willing to give his time and talents to others.

We would all do well to follow one of John Wesley's simple rules of conduct for living. He penned:

> *Do all the good you can,*
> *In all the ways you can,*
> *In all the places you can,*
> *At all the times you can,*
> *To all the people you can,*
> *As long as ever you can.*[6]

It seems appropriate that we should give of ourselves as a partial repayment for all we receive. "After all," said a spiritual leader, "we owe a kind of rent...or at least an obligation—for the space we occupy on earth, for the tenancy and tenure we have here, for the beauty and the sustenance, and the privilege of living life."[7]

If life seems to have lost some of its sparkle, perhaps it is because we are so involved in our own personal affairs that we have forgotten to reach out to others. But we should also be cautious of giving service at the expense of our own needs. "The ideal of altruistic virtue," as it has been called, can be carried too far. It is self-evident that we must care for our own welfare if we are going to be of service to others. Total disregard of others would be fatal to society, but at the same time, we must not forego our responsibility to ourselves. A doctor cannot be of service to his patients if he is unwell himself, nor can we be of help to others if we neglect our own lives.

Meaningful service to others can be provided in many ways and in varying degress, according to our individual abilities and talents. The widow's mite is just as significant as the rich man's fortune. We should serve our fellowmen in whatever way we can. As Longfellow once said, "Give what you have. To some one, it may be better than you dare to think."[8]   FEBRUARY 24, 1974

"I Am Only One"

Everyone we meet in life is an individual, and if there is nothing more to be said of a person, that is enough to warrant our attention. As a clergyman once stated, "I am only one/But still I am one:..."[9]

We are all somebody; but we are all as different as the stars in the heavens—different in talents and capacity, in judgment and inclination, in courage and temperament. This variety in people adds interest and challenge to life. It is the reason we must seek and recognize the worth of each individual. John Stuart Mill wrote, "The worth of a State in the long run is the worth of the individuals composing it."[10]

In referring to a church assignment, a good friend once paraphrased a well-known business slogan. "People," he said, "are our most important product." Our lives and associations revolve around people. People are the reason most of us do the things we do and it is each person's worth as an individual and as a child of our Father in heaven that is meaningful to our existence.

One of the important lessons teachers and leaders in all fields need to remember is the value of the individual. As A. M. Sullivan put it, "Man is still the most engaging syllable in management."[11] "The real art of management is understanding men—not just as statistics, or as parts of a large whole, but as individuals."[12]

This advice applies to us all. We must try to understand and be concerned with the lives of those we touch and try to remember that every individual is different, that no two can be treated alike. What makes one man happy may have an opposite effect on another. One person's strength may be another person's weakness.

Every worthwhile program has usually been established to help people, but as Paul Dunn expressed it, "If we are not careful, it is very easy to put the mechanics of the program ahead of people."[13] To understand and believe in people should be one of our first priorities. We are all alike in one way—that is: we are all different. No matter who we are or what our station in life may be, we are unique individuals. We might be "only one," but still we are one.   APRIL 29, 1973

Our Second Language

Communication with our fellowmen is one of the most basic, and yet most difficult tasks we face. At one time or another, nearly everyone experiences some frustration in communicating his ideas and feelings. Yet much of our success or failure can be attributed to how well we communicate.

Personal communication is a multifaceted function which involves more than just the words we speak or write. Our actions, our expressions, our grooming habits, even the clothes we wear are constantly communicating messages to those around us. In fact, they "speak" so loudly at times that one writer has labeled them our "second language."[14]

We face a double challenge in understanding and using this second language. First, there is a responsibility on our part to transmit only those messages we actually want to communicate. Most of us would probably be surprised at what we often "say" to others through our dress or mannerisms. As Emerson said, "When the eyes say one thing, and the tongue another, a practised man relies on the language of the first."[15] We are reading a second language when we cheer for a player because of the color of his uniform. And like the athlete, people often judge the goals in life we are aiming for by the "colors" we are wearing.

Secondly, we must try to be understanding, to show a sympathetic or tolerant attitude toward others. They, too, may not mean what they seem to be saying with their second language. Just because a person is wearing a ski parka does not necessarily mean he is a skier. It is incumbent upon each of us to withhold final judgment of an individual until we are confident that we have established accurate communication with him.

Now these forms of wordless communication are an important and useful part of life and influence us more than we may realize. A policeman's uniform, for example, communicates a message to society of assistance, just as the image of a man with a mask and a gun warns us of possible danger. Experiments have shown that pedestrians are more likely to follow a well-dressed person who crosses against the traffic light than one who is poorly dressed. Thus, we sometimes "listen" to another's "hidden" communication without realizing it.

And so we need ask ourselves "What is our message?" and "How are we sending it?" If we become more aware of the ways we are transmitting our thoughts and feelings, then perhaps we will also become more understanding of another person's communication. JULY 7, 1974

6

THE MIRACLE OF NATURE

nature | environment | pollution

sounds | private property

food and good health

*This earth of ours
is indeed a place of beauty.
Let us notice it,
appreciate it, and...
do what we can to preserve it.*

54

The Miracle of Nature

As spring returns each year, we are reminded of the hand of God in all things. The renewal of the land reveals and emphasizes His laws of nature at work. Indeed, spring, summer, autumn and winter—and all that occurs within the seasons—are not events that happen haphazardly. They are part of God's plan—some of which we understand, while some remain a mystery.

But this we can be sure of, that "There is a law, irrevocably decreed in heaven...upon which all blessings are predicated—And when we obtain any blessing from God, it is by obedience to that law upon which it is predicated."[1]

Now, one of the great blessings we enjoy is the miracle of nature. But this miracle is only possible through obedience to the law upon which it is predicated. If we want vegetables in summer, we must plant seeds in spring; if we want grass, we must provide water.

These are laws. To ignore them will be to deny our own blessings. And so it is with all natural things around us—our mountains, lakes and streams; the meadows, parks and flowers. They exist for our enjoyment as long as we do not interfere unwisely with God's laws of nature which make them possible.

It is also evident that these principles go far beyond mountains and seashores. If we want clean sidewalks in our cities, we must keep our refuse and litter contained. "Pollution is the twentieth-century word which simply means interfering with the natural cycles of nature. And it is not a word reserved only for business and industry. Most of us are guilty of contributing to the pollution of our environment. Therefore, we are all capable of contributing to the protection of our world by understanding and upholding the laws of nature. Clean air, clean water and clean streets begin with each of us.

If a healthful, pollution-free environment is what we want, then we must help nature keep the laws which make it possible, for, as recorded in Proverbs, "...he that keepeth the law, happy is he."[2]

MAY 19, 1974

The Possessions We Share With Others

Nearly all of us enjoy our public parks and recreation areas. And we enjoy them most when they are clean and well kept. But as the population increases and public property becomes more limited and crowded, there is an increasing need for us to take care of our recreation areas.

A well-known commentator[3] recently discussed the merits of public versus private property, pointing out that we are usually more likely to take care of our private possessions than our public ones. Because we have not proven our willingness to take care of that which we share with others, there is today a steadily increasing amount of public property becoming private—land which was at one time open and accessible to all.

When we're on the outside of the fence looking in, the signs which read "Private Property—Keep Out" do not radiate much warmth. They seem to say "Stay away— You're not our kind." But then, those who put up such signs probably do so because they have seen the way people treat public property. They have seen where citizens have littered, damaged and even destroyed public property. And if we think otherwise, we need only to scan a beach, park or campground after the crowd has gone.

It is ironic that many of the people who leave debris scattered behind after an outing are often the ones who take pride in their own immaculate homes and yards. Obviously they make a distinction between personal possions and those they share with others.

The same commentator remarked: I wonder how these people would react if I stood in front of their homes and littered their yards? They'd be furious.[3] And rightfully so, for no one has a right to destroy another's property. But we do have a responsibility to care for that which also belongs to others. Hopefully, we will remember this where-ever we go.

JUNE 10, 1973

An Old-Fashioned Walk

If we look for it, we can usually find something good and beneficial in any circumstance—even in the midst of adversity. And so, perhaps it would be well for us to look for the good that can come from what has been dubbed "the world energy crisis."

Some resulting good may be a slower pace of living, better planning, and less waste. On a personal level, one benefit each of us may take advantage of is an increased incentive to walk.

America's mobility is the envy of all mankind. For the most part it has been good. It has greatly broadened our horizons, allowed us a more comprehensive perspective about the world, afforded us opportunities to learn of other people and other lands, and to do it all in less time and expense than ever before.

But in our rush to move from place to place, perhaps we can't see the trees for the forest.

By walking, we see more of the world closest to us. We can look at a tree, or a flower, or talk to a neighbor. Walking slows us down and lets us take a closer look at life. Whether we walk to work—if we're fortunate enough to live that near our employment—or to church, or to the neighborhood grocery, we'll discover new insights into what makes our world beautiful. Indeed, an old-fashioned walk can be a marvelous tonic.

And a family walk can do much to open clogged lines of communication. It provides that little pause which gives time for a question from children, or an answer from parents, or a discussion of a long-felt problem.

And let us not forget the physical benefits from walking. Most physicians agree that walking is a fine form of exercise—exercise we don't often get because of our modern way of living.

Still another advantage of an occasional walk is the opportunity it provides us to be alone with our thoughts, to sort out our problems and brush a few cobwebs from the corners of our minds. More than anything else we might do, a walk could be the means of solving a perplexing problem. Many of our great, creative thinkers claimed they could think best when walking.

Yes, the energy problem will undoubtedly affect each of us in many different ways—some bad and some good. Hopefully, we'll get all the good out of it we can. And if we're able, some of that good will be an occasional, contemplative walk.   DECEMBER 9, 1973

Health: A Spiritual and Temporal Blessing

Throughout history much has been written and said about the need to care for our physical bodies. And as we move toward the end of the twentieth century, the fact still remains that our health is indeed a precious possession, and that the responsibility for it belongs with each of us individually.

Modern medicine, health clinics and spas can help keep us in shape, but there is little that can be done if we are not willing to personally commit ourselves to a responsible program of personal health care.

There are three good reasons, among others, for being physically fit. First, bodily vigor becomes mental and moral vigor, and is therefore essential to our happiness. Second, we have a responsibility to those around us: we have no right to neglect our health and become a burden to ourselves, and perhaps to others. And third, the Lord taught us that our bodies are sacred, that "the Spirit of God dwelleth"[4] within, and that we should not let anything defile "the temple of God."[5]

The physical and spiritual care of our bodies is a constant, demanding task. It is more than getting enough sleep and proper food. An American educator recently pointed out that "we transgress when we abuse [our bodies] by drinking, smoking, using other dangerous drugs, overeating, not exercising properly and not getting sufficient rest. When we witness how people treat themselves physically," continued Gus Turbeville, "it is a wonder that mankind reaches his allotted three score and seven years as often as he does."[6]

It is also well to remember that health care, like anything else, must be undertaken in moderation. Fanaticism in any form dangerously upsets the balance of life. To spend too much time exercising is as harmful as never exerting ourselves at all. A truly healthy person is one who carefully balances his physical, mental and spiritual well-being into a fully integrated way of life.

Indeed, our bodies are the physical temples given us to house our eternal spirits and souls. Failure to give them proper care is like pouring clear, mountain water into a rusty can. The responsibility and reward of healthful living rests with each of us. "He who has health," states an old proverb, "has hope; and he who has hope has everything."[7]

FEBRUARY 10, 1974

59

Feast or Famine

There is one thing all living creatures have in common—the need for food to sustain life. Plants require one type and animals another. People have varying nourishment needs, for what is a delight to one is often poison to another. But whatever form our appetites take, the fact remains that we must all eat to survive.

There has been much talk recently concerning the world food supply or the lack of it. We are all reminded—particularly at a holiday season—of the blessing of abundance for some and of the famine for others. Unfortunately, when an individual lacks food, the deficiency also carries over into other areas. It does little good to talk to a man of freedom when all he can think of is the emptiness of his stomach. As American writer O. Henry observed, "Love and business and family and religion and art and patriotism are nothing but shadows of words when a man's starving."[8]

None of us can change the world food situation by ourselves. But perhaps we can have an impact collectively, through wise and proper control of our appetites. And we would offer these suggestions as a beginning:

> *Eat moderately. If we resist overeating, we will not only leave more food for others, but will improve our own health and well being. "Surfeit has killed many more men than famine."*[9]

> *Avoid waste. We must teach and practice frugality at home. There are few valid reasons for discarding food, yet we allow it to happen without a second thought.*

> *Select proper foods. Many of the things we eat and drink were never intended for man, yet we consume them to the detriment of our mental and physical health and a loss to others. It has been recently reported that millions*

of people could be fed each year with the grains used to produce alcoholic beverages. As one dietician stated, "If you wish to live for enlightenment and success...choose your food purposely, not merely to tickle the appetite."[10]

We must all learn to control our appetites—both our physical and emotional—not only for our own good but for the good of others. "Our appetites and passions are virtues to perpetuate life." wrote David O. McKay. "Prostitute them and you have the vilest of sins."[11] A proper appetite is a God-given gift. But like all other gifts, it was intended that it be kept in bounds. DECEMBER 1, 1974

Throw-Away People

Our material possessions are an important part of our lives: Our food, clothes, homes, cars, all are part of our standard of living. Some have more possessions than many of us could ever imagine, while others, unfortunately, are lacking to the same degree. And no matter what we have, we always seem to want more. But for the majority of us in this country, there is, or has been, ample supply for our needs—if not our wants. But as most of us are keenly aware, that condition will not always exist unless proper steps are taken to ensure it.

Some of the best scientific minds in the world have tackled these issues, many of them long before it became fashionable to do so. And certainly we have no simple answers to these complex problems, but we would repeat today one oft-mentioned shortcoming which seems to plague our society. It is wastefulness.

When we are in the mountains or on the sea—

wherever we are alone with the vastness of nature—it is difficult to understand that our natural resources are of limited supply. And when we look at our farms, ranches and factories, it is hard to believe that our life-style and standard of living could change.

But it is happening. Our natural resources are dwindling, the products of our farms and factories are limited. Part of the reason for the strain is the notion many of us have that there is no need to be frugal, no need to save or take care of anything because there is always more—there is an unending supply awaiting us.

We have become throw-away people. We throw away items that are still useful because of the dictates of fashion or desire. Often it is a simple lack of motivation which directs our wastefulness, for it is easier to replace than to repair.

Our wastefulness is most serious in the area of food. It has been said that the food wasted in America could easily feed starving millions in other lands.

Yes, we can all improve. We can all waste less. In fact, the type of waste we speak of—squandering, extravagant wastefulness—could be eliminated altogether. It takes only a willingness to be satisfied with what we have, a willingness to get by with a little less, a little more often. If we do not, we may find that "willful waste brings woeful want."[12]   OCTOBER 27, 1974

"Silence Is of Eternity"

It has been said that "Silence is the element in which great things fashion themselves together, that at length they may emerge, full-formed and majestic, into the daylight of life, which they are henceforth to rule."[13]

Our modern, mechanized world often makes it difficult to find silence, or, at the very least, some degree of quiet. We are inundated with noise. We are constantly surrounded with the sounds of modern transportation, of construction, and of industry and society. They are all a part of life but, nevertheless, they are often disturbing.

Usually there is even a lack of silence in our own homes. In fact, we become so accustomed to it that we often feel uncomfortable in a quiet room. We subconsciously feel compelled to turn on a radio, television or phonograph to provide us with background "noise."

Silence seems to make us nervous. We go to extremes to surround ourselves with dissonance and people, for we seem to be psychologically afraid of our thoughts. It is nearly impossible to sit quietly with friends, for as soon as a conversation lags or stops, the unnerving silence is broken with more dialogue.

Many of the sounds of life are meaningful and important, but silence can also offer benefits. Perhaps we need to learn the value of silence. "I have often regretted my speech," wrote a Latin author, "never my silence."[14]

Silence also provides us an opportunity for introspection. It has been practiced by many world leaders. Even Christ the Lord was often alone for long periods of time.

And another interesting note: It has been discovered that "decisions and observations made alone in managed solitude have an uncanny way of being one hundred percent right."[15] As Marcus Aurelius wrote, "For nowhere either with more quiet or more freedom from trouble does a man retire than into his own soul, particularly when he has within him such thoughts that by looking into them he is immediately in perfect tranquility."[16]

Indeed, silence is a great tool in our lives. It is often in silence that we communicate with God. As Carlyle pointed out, "Speech is of time, silence is of eternity."[17]

DECEMBER 8, 1974

The Sound of Music

Every Sunday for more than 43 years, the Salt Lake Mormon Tabernacle Choir has broadcast one of the great joys of life—the sound of music. Today the Choir celebrates its 125th anniversary. The group began singing in 1847, beneath a wooden bowery in Salt Lake City. Over the years thousands have belonged to the Choir and millions of notes have been sung, all in an effort to express the joys of life through song.

"Music," wrote Carlyle, "is well said to be the speech of angels; in fact, nothing among the utterances allowed to man is felt to be so divine. It brings us near to the Infinite."[18] One sacred writing states: "For...[the Lord] delighteth in the song of the heart; yea, the song of the righteous is a prayer unto...[Him] and it shall be answered with a blessing upon their heads."[19]

Music affects everyone. All of us have fond memories related to music—countless experiences brought quickly to mind by a simple melody. Music moves and motivates us, and often we know not why.

Music can be a powerful force for good, and it can gently inspire us to higher plateaus and happier living. Yet, just as subtly, there is music that can slowly corrode man's fiber. In the hands of some men, it has wrought much anguish and sorrow.

Perhaps the greatest virtue of music is its ability to communicate in the most universal language known to man. One does not always have to understand the words in order to get the message. Nor does one have to understand the musical mechanics in order for it to be meaningful. As Stokowski said, "...it is only necessary that one enjoys it."[20] Indeed, music is one of the simple pleasures of life which we can all enjoy and find companionship with.

In his poem, "The Song By the Way," Mexican diplomat Francisco De Icaza wrote that though he was a foreigner in many lands, he was never alone as long as he could sing. He concluded by saying:

> *Ah, sad indeed that pilgrim's lot*
> *Who goes alone all day,*
> *Nor has, for comrade of his march,*
> *A song along the way![21]*

We all have need for songs along the way. But we must be sure that they are melodies that will comfort, encourage and guide us along paths of righteousness; indeed, songs that will be a delight to the Lord.

AUGUST 27, 1972, THE NATIONAL AUDITORIUM, MEXICO CITY, MEXICO

The Art of Listening

The Savior has given us much counsel, and on one occasion told us, "He who hath ears to hear, let him hear."[22] It was a brief but powerful message, for too often too many of us do not hear because we fail to listen. Listening requires concentration. We may hear a noise but we must listen to the beauty of music. We may hear someone talking, but we must listen to what he has to say. And is there not a parent who has made the mistake of hearing his child while failing to listen?

Listening also plays a vital role in building our storehouse memories for future enjoyment. The sounds we mentally record today may be replayed in our memories tomorrow. One author expressed those memorable sounds this way:

> *Today I heard the laughter of children at play. Their voices filled the air almost like chimes…. Today I heard a mockingbird trilling out every single song he ever heard from his winged friends. I closed my eyes and in the trees I heard all the voices I've heard since childhood, and it took me through all the happy, breathless, precious times I loved so much.*

*Today I heard my mother's voice calling to me happily.
It was a good, strong, healthy voice that has called to
me courage, and hope and peace...*

*Today I heard my child's voice. I heard her singing, I
heard her praying, I heard her laughing and talking. I
heard her teasing and moving from place to place in all
the activities I love to see her in.*

*Now, even more than ever I realize how grateful I am
that God has given me the...faculty of hearing.*[23]

Yes, hearing is a great gift. And the ability to listen
should be developed while we are young so we will not
miss the continuing harvest of memories. For the years
pass quickly, and if we have not made the effort to listen
when we could, we may one day find that our memory
bank is empty when suddenly we're older.

NOVEMBER 11, 1973

The Beauty of Nature

From the diary of Anne Frank we read: "The best remedy
for those who are afraid, lonely, or unhappy is to go outside, somewhere where they can be quite alone with the
heavens, nature and God. Because only then does one feel
that all is as it should be...amidst the simple beauty of
nature."[24]

It is true. When we see things of beauty, especially
the beauty in nature, we are uplifted and inspired at seeing
and being a part of its wonder. Wordsworth said, "My
heart leaps up when I behold a rainbow in the sky."[25]

"A thing of beauty is a joy for ever:/Its loveliness
increases; it will never/Pass into nothingness;..."[26] When
John Keats wrote his narrative poem about the Greek myth
of Endymion, he indicated he wrote of beauty because
our souls are "continually uplifted by 'Some shape of
beauty.'"[27]

66

The beauty of nature is all around us, but what is needed is a keener awareness of it on our part. We are told, "Look for a lovely thing and you will find it."[28] And when we do find it, we will also find that our spirit has been uplifted because of it.

Now, we should not only seek to appreciate the beauty of nature, but we should also seek to protect and preserve it. After making this planet our home for thousands of years we are just now beginning to realize the importance of keeping our environment beautiful so that it will be a "joy forever." That is not an easy thing to do. Mother Nature is the master architect and there are few instances when man can improve upon her work. Most things in life that are offensive are fashioned by man. But if we are to preserve and enjoy natural beauty there must be a universal effort to do so.

Nature was created for man. "...the Lord hath created the earth that it should be inhabited; and he hath created his children that they should possess it."[29] But like everything else that has been created, over which man has dominion, it must not be abused or it will no longer be of any value. This earth of ours is indeed a place of beauty. Let us notice it, appreciate it, and then if we do, we will also sincerely do what we can to preserve it.   APRIL 30, 1972

7

IN THE CHURCHES OF AMERICA

religion | spirituality and prayer

*Our need for religion
and spiritual nourishment
is as essential as our need for
food and water.*

In the Churches of America

We all need an occasional reminder to "lift our eyes unto the hills," and to remember that our greatest source of strength comes from the Lord.

Indeed, He will preserve our souls forever, and guide and influence our secular lives if we will but heed His counsel. It is essential, therefore, that we maintain our perspective during times of uncertainty, that we remember who we are, where we came from, why we are here, and where we are going.

Our earthly existence is part of a greater plan, one which began long before our first breath of mortal life, and one which will continue long after our bodies return to dust.

We should be on our knees daily, giving thanks and seeking continued strength and guidance to help us through this sometimes difficult life. As one religious leader remarked, "He who makes a habit of sincere prayer and prays believing, will find his life noticeably and profoundly enriched and steadied. He will increase in tranquility and poise; he will have added courage and stamina. His physical, moral and spiritual attitude will indicate he is aware of the presence of a powerful Friend."[1]

A French philosopher has also reminded us that therein lies the strength of this great land called America. Wrote de Tocqueville:

> *I sought for the greatness and genius of America in her commodious harbors and her ample rivers, and it was not there.*
>
> *I sought for the greatness and genius of America in her fertile fields and boundless forests, and it was not there ...in her rich mines and her vast world commerce, and it was not there....in her public school system and her*

institutions of learning, and it was not there.

I sought for the greatness and genius of America in her democratic congress and her matchless constitution, and it was not there.

Not until I went into the churches of America and heard her pulpits flame with righteousness did I understand the secret of her genius and power.

America is great because America is good, and if America ever ceases to be good, America will cease to be great.   JANUARY 13, 1974

Our Most Important Natural Resource

No one will deny that the world in which we live is vastly different and more complex than that of our ancestors. It is also a rapidly changing world, and the problems of rapid growth and expansion are responsible, in part at least, for many of the crises we face.

As we seek the proper solution to these problems, it may be well to remember that gas, oil and coal are not our only natural resources; that there is available to us all a spiritual resource more powerful and of greater value than any of the material resources we are depleting. And more important, the only shortage in this spiritual well is the one we create by not drinking from it frequently.

It was this same spiritual strength which gave Moses power to lead the children of Israel, Abraham to obey the Lord at the risk of his son's life; and this same spiritual strength which gave the Savior the ability to heal the sick, walk on water, and overcome mortal death. "The Master's resources," wrote one essayist, "were entirely spiritual.

"The demand of our times, then, is that we begin to look beyond matter to the realm of God, [to the spiritual] for a true sense of inexhaustible substance and energy."[3]

If we are truly concerned about the difficulties facing the world, then we should not ignore the greatest natural resource available to us. As "faith without works is dead,"[4] so is work without faith. "A man who puts aside his religion because he is going into society," said Richard Cecil, "is like one taking off his shoes because he is about to walk upon thorns."[5]

Whatever our time in history, we must remember that our real strength in life comes from the Lord. We will solve our problems more effectively by seeking His guidance.

In ages past, spirituality may have been the only natural resource known to man. Today, however, with all that has been developed—much of it through the inspiration of the Lord—we have often the tendency, unfortunately, to forget from whence cometh our greatest help.

May we always remember that there is no substitute for spiritual strength. JANUARY 20, 1974

In the Early Morning

No part of the day provides greater promise or hope for the future than the early morning hours. It is a time when careful observation will reveal the progress of life. We are aware of the Earth's moving, the dew beginning to evaporate, the birds taking wing, animals stirring about and flowers opening to drink the morning sun. Indeed, morning is a time of testimony that God lives and that life is eternal.

71

Little wonder that a boy would seek God in a shady woodland beneath the radiant warmth of a morning sun. For although any time is a good time to seek God, the dawning of a new day seems to be especially appropriate for prayer.

Prayer is one of life's reassuring cornerstones. It should not—as some mistakenly suggest—be left exclusively to the clergy, for prayer is our channel of communication with our Creator, and no one is so self-sufficient that he can afford to pass up that opportunity.

There are also those who recognize the need for prayer, but feel they lack the ability. They, too, are in error, for everyone can communicate with God.

Today we would offer a few simple suggestions to remind us all of how to pray:

1. *Our approach should be simple and natural. We should talk to God as a child would talk to his parent, telling Him what's on our mind. There is no need for elaborate words or formality. Our Father will hear us if we speak plainly and with proper respect.*

2. *We must remember to acknowledge blessings already granted before seeking additional help for ourselves or others.*

3. *We must be honest and earnest. A facade is displeasing and of no value.*

4. *We should often pray audibly when we are alone— not loudly, but with a quiet utterance that helps define our thoughts and brings greater meaning to the concept of talking with God.*

5. *And finally, we must pray with faith. As one has written, there is no need to pray for God to come to us, for that prayer is answered before we give it.*

We are all soldiers in the battle of life. And it would be well for us to remember that prayer can help us meet the skirmishes ahead. Indeed, it can make the difference between victory and defeat. APRIL 6, 1975

A Desert Without Landmarks

There is a growing need in the world today for religious commitment. With few exceptions, church membership throughout the world is experiencing a general decline, a condition foretold in an early prophecy: "For behold, at that day shall he rage in the hearts of the children of men, and stir them up to anger against that which is good. And others will he pacify, and lull them away into carnal security, that they will say: All is well in Zion, yea,...all is well —and thus the devil cheateth their souls and leadeth them away carefully down to hell."[6]

Our need for religion and spiritual nourishment is as essential as our need for food and water. Alfred Noyes pointed out, "The universe is centered on neither the earth nor the sun. It is centered on God."[7]

Those who do not want religion often say it is because of a desire to be free—free from commitment, conscience and constraints. Certainly, as Morris West stated: Without the faith one has the pleasant feeling at first of being free. Yet, in reality, the opposite is true. One is only "free in chaos, in an unexplained and unexplainable world"[8] —like being in a desert without landmarks, where one can walk in any direction without knowing where he is headed, whether he is coming or going. It is true, we are then free, but lost in utter chaos.

A sociologist recently said there is a genuine quest for religion now under way among the young. He further added that after a generation of prosperity, it is not surprising to have our stomachs full but our souls empty.[9]

Indeed, man needs a basic measuring point in life, and religion can provide it. A theological framework will establish landmarks which can lead us to happiness and fulfillment. Commitment to religion is not restrictive when one examines the purpose of life, but rather, freeing.

DECEMBER 3, 1972

"More Things Are Wrought by Prayer..."

There seems little reason to doubt the truthfulness of Tennyson's observation that "More things are wrought by prayer/Than this world dreams of."[10] Indeed, more happens because of someone's unknown prayer than we will ever know.

It was once reported to one of this country's well-known spiritual leaders that prayer is the greatest power in the world. "It is a pity that more people do not know how to use it."[11] But even if we know how, what good is our knowledge if we do not use it?

There are those who doubt the power of prayer, who regard it as refuge for weaklings, or a childish petition for material things. There are others who acknowledge its usefulness but remain afraid or unwilling to use it themselves.

Responding to the first point, we offer this observation: In a world where millions can see and hear men walking on the moon, where light beams can be used to move objects, and where machines can see into places even the human eye cannot probe—in a world where all this is often a common occurrence, is it so difficult to believe that we have the power to communicate with our Creator?

"Prayer is a force as real as terrestrial gravity," said a prominent physician. "It is the only power in the world that seems to overcome the so-called laws of nature."[12] Certainly there should be no mystery about the possibility of prayer.

To those who believe but are reluctant to commit themselves to daily prayer, we would point out that prayer is not an exercise conjured up by religious leaders. It is a means of communication given to all mankind by our Father in heaven. It requires no special language, no special commission, only faith and a willingness to believe.

It has been well-documented that the Founding Fathers of this country used prayer in their quest for peace and freedom. And it was, undoubtedly, the same recourse to prayer, in the same quest for peace and freedom, that led thousands of joyful prisoners of war back to their homes and families.

If we are truly concerned about protecting that freedom, of having "amber waves of grain" and "purple mountain majesties," of "brotherhood from sea to shining sea," then let us turn to the greatest Power on earth. For it will only be through prayer that God can "shed his grace on thee."

> *O beautiful for spacious skies,*
> *For amber waves of grain,*
> *For purple mountain majesties*
> *Above the fruited plain!*
> *America! America!*
> *God shed his grace on thee*
> *And crown thy good with brotherhood*
> *From sea to shining sea!* [13]

FEBRUARY 18, 1973

75

"You Can't Pray a Lie"

Communication with God should have priority in our lives, for it is through prayer that we receive much of the strength and encouragement needed to combat adversity. Man has always struggled to survive and achieve, and those most successful have usually made prayer an integral part of their lives.

The Master taught that "whatsoever ye shall ask in prayer, believing, ye shall receive."[14] Often the things we most need is assurance concerning the decisions we must make—the kind of quiet confidence that can only come from the Lord.

Abraham Lincoln, whose life led him to the leadership of a struggling nation, said prayer was one of his great strengths. "I have been driven many times to my knees," he said, "by the overwhelming conviction that I had nowhere else to go. My own wisdom and that of all about me seemed insufficient for that day."[15] It is indeed true, as Tennyson observed, that "More things are wrought by prayer than this world dreams of."[16]

One of the basic elements of successful prayer is honesty—honesty with ourselves, honesty about our motives and our efforts. As Mark Twain's Huckleberry Finn said, "...I made up my mind to pray and see if I couldn't try...and be better...But the words wouldn't come...because my heart warn't right,...I was lettin' on to give up sin, but...inside of me I was holdin' on to the biggest one of all. I was tryin' to make my mouth say [what]...was a lie and He [knew] it. You can't pray a lie."[17]

Along with honesty, successful prayer also requires some degree of personal responsibility. Pioneer leader Brigham Young advised his followers to do all in their power to overcome difficulties before turning to the Lord. To do otherwise, he said, would be as illogical as asking "the Lord to cause [the] wheat and corn to grow without ...plowing the ground and casting the seed."[18] And he added that we should "pray as if all depended upon the Lord, and work as if all depended upon [us]."[18]

Yes, prayer can be a powerful tool in our lives, for when we lift our soul unto the Lord, we suddenly realize that He is our strength and our hope.   FEBRUARY 2, 1975

The Yearning for a Spiritual Home

"O for a closer walk with God."[19] Yes, we would all benefit from a close "everyday" relationship with our Father in heaven, but too often we walk with Him only on the Sabbath or on special occasions. And that is not enough. It is a simple, but proven, religious principle that life's burdens become lighter when we build a strong, personal, daily association with God.

Whether we are religious or not, most of us in our journey through life experience what Beatrice Webb called "a yearning for the mental security of a spiritual home."[20] Such a spiritual home gives us the strength we need when we need it most. The pressures and difficulties which occur in each of our lives do not conveinently confront us only when we are prepared to meet them—only when we are ready for difficulties. They come any hour, any day, often when we are least prepared; and if we have not built into our lives a daily, close association with God, then the comfort and guidance which come from such living will not be ours. Harry Emerson Fosdick pointed out that we need deep resources if we are to come through such times unembittered, unspoiled, and still a real person.[21]

Such deep resources come through daily prayer and a growing relationship with our Father in heaven. It is always easier to communicate and seek advice from a "friend" with whom we walk daily. That same concept has been stressed throughout history. Some eighteen hundred years ago Marcus Aurelius wrote, "Man must be arched and buttressed from within..."[22] And Abraham Lincoln added just a century ago, "Find out the way that God is going and go that way."[23]

Our challenge is to develop a spiritual philosophy that will help us meet the problems of life, and sustain us through the dark hours that inevitably come to all of us. Our challenge is to walk closer with God.   APRIL 15, 1973

Religion and Sports

At no other time in history has the interest and devotion to sports been as high as it is today, especially in the United States. Oh, there may have been fans more rabid or participants more devoted at various times in the past, for various events, but on the whole, more people are now enjoying some form of athletic activity than ever before.

The attraction reaches a high point in the fall and spring of the year when many of the most popular sports overlap. In the crisp autumn air, for instance, football is under way, baseball play-offs and basketball are beginning, hunting and fishing are at their best, and most other activities, from golf to tennis, continue to attract attention.

For the most part this is good. For the fans it provides exciting entertainment. Some sports, such as football, are great seasonal rituals, adding to community life. And for the participants, in all sports, it means added self-discipline and confidence, increased physical prowess, and the healthy exercise of competitive spirit.

Recreational sports have been with us for a long time. The Lord has always been an advocate of physical as well as spiritual strength, of a healthy body as well as a sound mind. In this sense, the interest in sports has been good for the nation; indeed, good for the world.

But, as in all good things, there is a need for moderation and responsibility in our recreational pursuits. If some unknowing visitor came to the United States between September and April, he could easily conclude that the national "religion" is football or basketball. Unfortunately, they have, in fact, become the only "worship" service many persons attend.

Writer Harry Edwards carries the analogy one step further. He says: "Sport manifests every characteristic of a formal, thriving religion movement; it has its gods (super-star athletes),...its scribes (the hundreds of sportscasters [and writers]...), its houses of worship (the Astrodome and other facilities that rival anything ever constructed to house traditional worship services). And sport has one other feature that traditional religion has long since lost in American society—massive throngs or highly vocal,...'true believers'..."[24]

No, there is nothing wrong with sports. They provide some of the great enjoyments of life. But they will do so only as long as we maintain our perspective and do not let them replace our "religion." SEPTEMBER 30, 1973

"A Blessing to Enjoy"

If there is one assurance we have it is the knowledge that this life, as we know it, will end for each of us. To many that is a frightening and disturbing thought. To others, as the author of the song portrays, it is a precious moment in the sight of the Lord.[25]

What an exciting and humbling experience it will be to stand before our Maker and discuss our accomplishments and failures of this earth-test.

But we must not forget that the opportunity to speak to the Lord is a blessing for which we don't have to wait until we are called home to enjoy. In His superior wisdom, the Lord knew we would need His guidance and inspiration to help us through the trials and temptations of this life, so He gave us prayer.

Prayer is not an exercise performed for the benefit of those around us. It is a duty enjoined by the command of God and a means of communicating directly with our Father in heaven. We would probably spend more time praying if we recognized that prayer is a blessing to enjoy, not something that needs to be taken care of.

And so often we say our prayers, but we do not pray. Praying is more than just saying words. It is a pouring out of the soul to God. As the King said in Shakespeare's *Hamlet*," My words fly up, my thoughts remain below: Words without thoughts never to heaven go."[26]

Prayer should be an earnest and humble petition from the heart; an honest, sincere supplication of our righteous desires; not some complex, glorified celebration of trite and meaningless words.

And, of course, prayer must be supported with faith and action. As "faith without works is dead..."[27] so prayer without faith and works is also of little value. Prayer was given to us as a useful tool, not as a simple substitute for that which we could do for ourselves. A spiritual leader once pointed out that prayer "will add a dimension to [our] lives which can come from no other source and which will give [us] wealth beyond expression."[28]

It takes a willingness on our part to lift our eyes unto the mountain from whence cometh our help,[29] and a fine tuning of our spiritual self in order that we might hear the soft and subtle answers. MARCH 3, 1974

Prayer...A Constant Habit

An oft-quoted line from those returning from war says: "There are no atheists in foxholes." And, I suppose we could add, as The Navy Hymn suggests, nor are there any atheists on sinking ships or in troubled aircraft.

When we become frightened, when we become anxious about the future, and certainly when our lives are in danger, we turn to the Creator for help and guidance. What joy and comfort it is to know that there is One to whom we can turn in time of need.

"I have been driven many times to my knees," said Lincoln, "by the overwhelming conviction that I had nowhere else to go."[15] And so it is with us all when we have nowhere else to go.

But what of those times when all is going well, when the decisions we make seem to be the right ones, when there appears little need for help? Are we as likely then to turn to Him? "Conversation with God," someone said, "should be a constant habit, not a maddened plea when one is at wit's end."[30]

When life is going smoothly it is easy to forget Him from whom all blessings flow. In this jet-age world, there are many of us who feel the need for constant prayer, but who don't take the time. And if we don't take the time —or worse, if we don't find the need for prayer when all is well, perhaps in times of trouble we may feel so out of touch, so out of practice, such a stranger in the art of communicating with the Lord, that we'll lack the faith, indeed, even the knowledge of how to pray. "...Pray always, and be believing," it is written, "and all things shall work together for your good...."[31]

Prayer should not be an emergency measure to be used as we would a spare tire when we have a flat, but rather to be used as a steering wheel in guiding our destiny.

Gibran wrote, "You pray in your distress and in your need; would that you might pray also in the fullness of your joy and in your days of abundance."[32]   MARCH 26, 1972

8

"COME, FOLLOW ME"

God | the Lord Jesus Christ | the Savior,

God's Commandments and Eternal Life

And this is life eternal,
that they might know thee the only true God,
and Jesus Christ, whom thou hast sent.

JOHN 17: 3

To know the Christ
is the duty of us all,
and not alone our duty,
but our privilege.

J. REUBEN CLARK, JR.

"Come, Follow Me"

Of all the precepts taught by the Savior none was of fewer words, yet more difficult to live, than His simple admonition to come, "follow me."[1] Indeed, to follow the teachings and example of the Savior is a great challenge, and the reward is everlasting. As the Lord Himself pointed out "...this is my work and my glory—to bring to pass the immortality and eternal life of man."[2]

We all seek, or should seek, eternal life. Preparation for it is our purpose on earth, and the only way this goal can be achieved is through Jesus Christ. Remember the words of His prayer on the way to Gethsemane, "And this is life eternal, that they might know thee the only true God, and Jesus Christ, whom thou hast sent."[3] One wise diplomat and spiritual leader pointed out, "To know the Christ is the duty of all of us, and not alone our duty, but our privilege;..."[4]

Unfortunately, one of the goals we probably lose sight of more than any other is our own individual salvation. We become so involved with life that we overlook its purpose; we fail to understand what it is all about. Rightfully, we should be concerned with education and occupation, with marriage and parenthood, with recreation and leisure—all the important activities which fill our days. But sometimes we forget that all of them are a part of the Savior's challenge to us. Indeed, the sum total of all we do in life will determine our final grade.

The final examination in this great eternal school begins the day we are born. Some of us may have nearly finished it, others may be just beginning. None of us know exactly where we are for it varies with each individual. However, one thing is certain: It is the most important examination we will ever take and no makeups will be allowed.

Our opportunity to follow the Savior is *now*, for we never know what temptation, or challenge, or experience awaits us; but if we always remember why we are here, why the Savior invited us to follow Him—that is, to earn our own salvation—then we will be less likely to be caught in one of life's pitfalls.   APRIL 8, 1973

"The Light of Life"

One of man's greatest fears is fear of the unknown. When children, or even adults, fear the dark, it is because of what they cannot see. Part of the anxiety parents experience in rearing a family comes during the hours they wait and wonder if their children will return home safely. Often the worst moments in war, earthquakes and other disasters are those when we cannot forsee the immediate future. The concern on the faces of those in a hospital waiting room mirrors the fear of what they do not yet know. It is not knowing what lies ahead that is often the most agonizing part of an experience.

It is, therefore, quite understandable why so many express a fear of death—a fear which does not come from the experience itself, but from not knowing what lies beyond. It is the fear of the unknown. In this sense, they are like children in a dark room, afraid because they are without light—without the light of life.

Fortunately, the Light of Life was sent to man centuries ago, bringing peace, understanding and assurance to those who will listen:

> *In the beginning was...God...In him was life; and the life was the light of men. And the light shineth in darkness; and the darkness comprehended it not.* [5]

85

Then spake Jesus again unto them, saying, I am the light of the world: he that followeth me shall not walk in darkness, but shall have the light of life.[6]

What greater comfort could the Savior offer than to light the way past the unknown. But, of course, to walk in the light requires effort on our part. The light is there if we are willing to follow it. It will not only eliminate fear of the future, but will reduce many of the anxieties we face in everyday living. The light of Christ is truly the light of life, and through Him we will find "Unto the upright there ariseth [a] light in the darkness."[7]   JULY 30, 1972

"A Closer Walk With God"

As we approach the New Year our thoughts turn to all that has transpired in the past few months, and we cannot help but wonder and be a little concerned about what lies ahead. But with all our wondering, one thought must remain paramount: that God lives and is standing nearby to calm and comfort us in time of need.

I suppose we all yearn at times for a closer walk with God; yearn for the peace which comes from being near our Master.

Recently this choir and millions of people the world over were shocked and saddened at the sudden death of a man dear to us all. If ever there was a man amongst us who walked close to God it was Harold B. Lee. Now he is gone. But we can take from his own writings some advice that might help us through this coming year: "What can we say," he wrote, "to those who are yearning for an inward peace to quiet their fears, to ease the aching hearts, to bring understanding, to look beyond the sordid trials of today and see the fruition of hopes and dreams in a world beyond mortality?

"May I call attention," he continued, "to the promises in the scriptures...that...bring understanding, peace and hope."[8] And then he quoted from the Master, "Peace I leave with you, my peace I give unto you: not as the world giveth, give I unto you. Let not your heart be troubled, neither let it be afraid."[9]

The peace spoken of by the Master, and the comfort we so much seek cannot be found in material wealth or an abundance of goods. It exists only in the individual hearts of men and women, and it is only there that one can be close to his Maker.

Now there are those who might doubt God's existence, and therefore refuse themselves the benefit of God's greatest gifts—comfort in this earthly existence and joy in the eternal life to come.

In commenting on the existence of God, Thomas Edison once used an analogy which might be even more fitting today. "We don't know what electricity is," he said. "We don't know what heat is.... But we do not let our ignorance about these things deprive us of their use."[10] Nor should we allow any lack of understanding about God deprive us of His blessings. Yes, He does live and is willing to help us even if we don't have a perfect knowledge of Him.

May we all find greater peace and comfort this coming year through a closer walk with God

DECEMBER 30, 1973

May Peace Be With You...

There is no peace in the world more comforting than that which the Savior spoke of when He said, "Peace I leave with you, my peace I give unto you."[11] It was the Master's last discourse to His apostles before His crucifixion, and He assured them that God lives, that life would go on, that they would not be left without comfort (even the great Comforter, the Holy Ghost), and that happiness and serenity that comes through keeping His commandments would be theirs. Such was the peace Christ promised to His apostles. Such is the peace available to us all.

For many years this program has closed with words of the late Richard Evans, "May peace be with you, this day—and always." Occasionally someone will ask what peace we speak of? I think it safe to say it is the peace of Christ; the quiet comfort and strength which come only through an understanding of the purpose of life; the assurance that God lives, and that we can find eternal happiness through a willing obedience to His commandments.

But peace in any form is desirable. Joseph Conrad wrote "...what all men are really after is some form or perhaps only some formula of peace."[12] But too often the peace we seek is not a lasting one, or is a peace sought for the wrong reasons or in the wrong places. It has been said, "When a man finds no peace within himself it is useless to seek it elsewhere."[13] And Emerson added, "Nothing can bring you peace but yourself; nothing can bring you peace but the triumph of principles."[14] It is the triumph of the principles Christ taught that will bring us the most worthwhile peace.

And we would add this final comment: If all mankind would embrace the peace He left us, all other forms of peace would follow as surely as night follows day. As Paul told the Philippians, "...the peace of God, which passeth all understanding shall keep your hearts and minds through Christ Jesus."[15] Such is the peace He left us. Such is the peace we should seek "this day—and always."   JANUARY 26, 1975

"Lead Thou Me On"

One of the most peaceful, reassuring times in life is when we are tramping alone in the woods. The quiet wonder of nature assures us there is a Supreme Being, One far greater than us whose plan is eternal and everlasting, One who would have us find true joy and happiness through obedience to His laws and commandments.

Keeping on course by following the commandments of God is much like hiking in the woods. When we know where we are and where we are going, there is no need to fear and we can enjoy our surroundings. But when we are lost and alone with no guideposts to follow, panic overtakes us; we see no beauty in anything and even become destructive of ourselves and our surroundings in an attempt to survive.

Life itself is much like that. When there is love in our hearts for God and our fellowmen, when we are honest with ourselves, and when we do those things the Lord has told us to do, there is a serenity and happiness within our souls that cannot be defeated. But when we fail to keep the commandments, a sense of guilt, uneasiness and lack of confidence creeps into our character. And what is worse, we are usually not aware of it until it is too late. When all is going well, we feel self-sufficient—like knowing where we are in the woods. But when difficulty arises that we cannot cope with, we become lost and suddenly find we are in need of God but know not where to find Him.

Where there is imperfect knowledge, faith is of prime importance. The Lord did not promise to make *all* things known unto us, but He did promise to give us sufficient knowledge for our needs. In times like these we could easily have the feeling of being lost, and of wondering how and when we will ever solve our problems. What

is needed is less panic and despair, and more faith and
belief in the commandments of God.

John Henry Newman expressed it best in these
lyrics:

> *"Lead, kindly Light, amid the encircling gloom,*
> *Lead Thou me on!*
> *The night is dark, and I am far from home;*
> *...I do not ask to see*
> *The distant scene; one step enough for me.*
> *...Lead Thou me on!"[16]*
>
> MARCH 10, 1974

"I Know That
My Redeemer Lives"

More meaning and happiness has been given to mankind
through the life of Jesus Christ than by any other individual. He showed us the way to salvation and exaltation.
He gave us life everlasting, and He taught us, through both
word and deed, the requirements for peace and happiness.
Indeed, we owe much to the Master, and one of the best
ways we can repay Him is to develop a firm faith in what
He taught. Those who do believe and follow His teachings
have what many call a testimony—a deep and abiding conviction of the divinity of the Savior.

A testimony is like a cornerstone. It gives strength
and meaning to life. It tells us—and those around us—
where we stand. It gives us a solid base upon which to
build a more satisfying life. A man without a knowledge
and testimony of God is a wanderer. His spirit is not rooted
in the solid soil of understanding, and his potential for
meaningful growth is limited. We all need that foundation
which a testimony gives, that rock of knowledge upon
which faith and self-confidence can build.

Such a conviction does not begin with a perfect,
absolute knowledge. Were it so there would be little need
for faith, and God's plan of salvation would have little

90

meaning. A true belief or testimony of what is meaningful comes to both the mind and the heart. It is a spiritual and intellectual experience available to all who will allow it to happen.

A wise physician counsels young people who may doubt the need or even the possibility of acquiring a testimony of God: Experiment with it, he advises, for two months, six months or a year. Attend church meetings, give up any bad habits you may have, try to associate with people who have high moral values, let your religious leaders know you want to be involved, and don't forget to pray. Live sincerely, and with all your heart, strive to find the truth. Then the Lord, by the Holy Spirit, will give you a testimony. It's that simple—not easy, mind you, but simple.[17]

And it is good advice for us all. A testimony of the Lord *can* be acquired and it *can* also be lost. And so the need for us to heed the wisdom of the Lord. If we will but do as He instructs, we too will be able to testify along with countless others, "I know that my Redeemer lives."

APRIL 7, 1974

"...For Always and Forever"

Nearly two thousand years ago Mary Magdalene, Joanna, and Mary, the mother of James, stood with others before a huge, rock cave which was being used as a tomb—and found it empty. Already they had suffered extreme grief and misery, and then an added disappointment. But soon they, and millions of others since, learned that their disappointment was not another cruel injustice by men, but rather the greatest event in history: the resurrection of Jesus Christ.[18]

As they stood wondering what had happened to the body of their Master who just hours before had been crucified, two angels appeared and said unto them, "Why seek ye the living among the dead? He is not here, but is risen."[18] And later Christ did appear as a resurrected being before His disciples. So, for the first time, mortal men knew that life did not end at the grave, that life is eternal, and that this earthly existence is only another step along the eternal path of progression.

When we lose a loved one, close friend or associate, we are sorrowed at the immediate loss, but we can find peace and comfort in knowing that this is not the end, that separations are not permanent, that life has only arrived at another milestone; that life goes on.

Not many months ago this broadcast lost a long-time associate, one responsible for this sermonette for over forty years. Just three months before Richard Evans' death, he spoke at the funeral service of a dear friend—one who, for over half a century, was a member of the Tabernacle Choir. On this occasion, Richard L. Evans expressed his great feeling of the resurrection and everlasting life.

"If I thought," he said, "that at some moment of accident or illness all would be as if it has never been; if I thought that each morning would bring me one day closer to the end of associations with our four sons and their beautiful mother, I would wonder if life meant much; I would wonder if the Creator knew His business? But, blessedly, He hasn't planned that way for us, but has given us the assurance that life, and loved ones, and truth and intelligence, personality, and the sweetness of association with loved ones, and with our Father, are planned for always and forever."[19]

Indeed, the eternal life of man is made by the gift and sacrifice of Jesus Christ.

> *I am the resurrection, and the life; he that believeth in me, though he were dead, yet shall he live;*
> *And whosoever liveth and believeth in me shall never die."*[20]

APRIL 2, 1972

9

THE POWER THAT MOVES TO ACTION

faith | conviction and hope

*Faith in itself is
not the solution to our problems,
but it is the means
by which we can overcome
our fears and doubts,
our disappointment and despair;
the means by which
we can find the courage to
go forward in life
and solve our problems.*

93

The "Power That Moves to Action"

As we ponder life and the problems that face us every day, we are ofttimes stunned at what seems to be a lack of solutions to our problems. As we look to our future—especially the young—we could easily become discouraged and filled with despair at its prospects.

We are constantly being warned of the dangers man is imposing upon himself. And young people often get the impression that the future is bleak, that there are too many insolvable problems, too many questions without answers.

Sometimes we don't know the answers and have to accept life on faith. Someone said, "It has taken me all my life to understand that it is not necessary to understand everything."[1]

The late American statesman, John Foster Dulles, said: "We are establishing an all-time world record in the production of material things. What we lack is a righteous and dynamic faith."[2] What we need to assure our future is a faith in life, a faith in God. Sometimes because we lack faith, we are driven to act in ways we know are wrong, actions that we would not ordinarily attempt under different circumstances.

Now faith in itself is not the solution to our problems, but it is the means by which we can overcome our fears and doubts, our disappointment and despair; the means by which we can find the courage to go forward in life and solve our problems.

David O. McKay offered this observation and guidance: "[Faith] is more than a mere feeling. It is power that moves to action, and should be in human life the most basic of all motivating forces.... The great need of today is faith that will put purpose into life, and courage into the

94

heart.... The need of the world is more than a mere acceptance of [Jesus Christ] as the greatest of all men. What is really essential is faith in Him as a divine being—as our Lord and Savior."[3]

Faith is like climbing a hill when one is lost. From the canyons below it is nearly impossible to tell which direction to turn, but when we reach the crest, we can see the road below and where it leads, and feel assured that we are going in the right direction and will reach our destination. And so it is with faith.

"Faith is the assurance of things hoped for, the conviction of things not seen."[4] As Emerson expressed it, "All I have seen teaches me to trust the Creator for all I have not seen."[5]

APRIL 9, 1972

The Need for Hope

"Not all lost then was our hope,/Our proud hope so old yet new..."[6] These phrases from *Hatikva*, a Hebrew word meaning "the hope," express a feeling that though much may have been lost, there is still hope—a new, revitalized hope.

Hope is "the only good that is common to all men," wrote a Greek philosopher. "Those who have nothing else, possess hope still."[7]

Disappointment and frustration result when we cannot realize our hopes. But the challenge of hope is to exert oneself to effort or activity when life seems most hopeless.

Former U. S. President Lyndon Johnson said, "Unfortunately, many [people] live on the outskirts of hope.... Our task is to help replace their despair with opportunity."[8]

We have a moral responsibility not only to cherish our own hopes and dreams, but to be concerned and aware of the hopes and dreams—and needs—of those around us.

95

From a prayer, we read, "[Help us] that we may neither grow proud through success, nor become embittered by failure. May we sympathize with those whose hopes have been disappointed and whose labors have been unfruitful."[9]

When we build our hopes, let us knit them together with the hopes of others; let us search for that which is righteous, wholesome and uplifting; let us hope for peace, love and happiness; for character, wisdom and understanding.

Wilferd Peterson summed it up this way:

> The well-known maxim, "While there is life, there is hope," has deeper meaning in reverse: "While there is hope, there is life." Hope comes first, life follows. Hope gives power to life. Hope rouses life to continue to expand, to grow, to reach out, to go on. Hope sees a light where there isn't any. Hope lights candles in millions of despairing hearts.[10]

Where there is hope, there is life.   APRIL 16, 1972

Faith to Combat Fears

There are many people in the world who do not know where the path they follow will lead nor where it will end. To some extent we are all that way, for no one knows exactly what the future has in store. But some walk the path more comfortably than others because they follow the route of the Savior.

One of the reasons the Savior came to earth was to chart the course for us; to mark out that pathway. He gave directions, warned of obstacles, and taught that faith was paramount in completing the journey. He taught us of eternity and its rewards for the faithful, but left us to develop a conviction of its reality by ourselves—through faith.

Recently we spoke of the need to avoid fear and the panic it can create. Faith can combat those fears, as Harry Emerson Fosdick once pointed out: "Fear imprisons, faith liberates"; he said, "fear paralyzes, faith empowers; fear disheartens, faith encourages; fear sickens, faith heals; …and, most of all, fear puts hopelessness at the heart of life, while faith rejoices in its God."[11] And, wrote another, "Fear and lack of faith go hand in hand. The one is born of the other."[12]

One of the more comforting feelings we can experience in life is to know where we are and where we are going. Faith can provide that comfort and give us a deep understanding of life's purpose. Without faith in the future the present has little meaning.

These words by Eliza R. Snow exemplify the faith needed to understand our purpose in life and its promise for the future:

> *"Oh my Father…When shall I regain thy presence, And again behold thy face?…For a wise and glorious purpose, Thou has placed me here on earth and withheld the recollection of my former friends and birth.… I had learned to call thee, Father…But until the key of knowledge Was restored, I knew not why.… When I leave this frail existence,…when I've completed All you sent me forth to do, With your mutual approbation, Let me come and dwell with you."[13]* JULY 15, 1973

"If Ye Have Faith…"

When the Savior taught His manner of prayer during the Sermon on the Mount, He did so with the understanding that man would also exercise the faith required to realize his desires. Although it may be nothing more than a strong belief for some, it is through faith that we are able to accomplish much of what we do.

Shortly after His transfiguration, Christ was asked by His disciples why they could not heal a sick child as He had done. And Jesus answered: "Because of your unbelief: for verily I say unto you, If ye have faith as a grain of mustard seed, ye shall say unto this mountain, Remove hence to yonder place; and it shall remove; and nothing shall be impossible unto you."[14]

What an inspiring challenge to know that "nothing shall be impossible." We all have that potential. "Anyone can move a mountain," wrote Johnny Marks.[15] Of course, there are degrees of ability and faith. One artist may paint a picture with relative ease, while another must exert much effort and exercise great faith. Likewise, keeping the commandments of God may be a simple task for one individual and a difficult matter for another, even though the desires of both may be just as great and just as sincere.

Some may argue against trying to achieve those things which require faith—trying to overcome the personal mountains we face each day. But our desires and dreams will never be realized unless we include the prime ingredient—faith—which turns them into reality. Without faith we are like the disciples of old who wanted to heal the child but could not.

Faith is the elixir of youth. Whoever has faith is young, no matter how old he is; whoever has lost faith is old, even at twenty-one. Faith will turn any course, light any path, relieve any distress, bring joy out of sorrow and peace out of strife. The need for faith never leaves us. We should never forget that faith, even as little as a tiny grain of mustard seed, will allow us to move a mountain.

AUGUST 6, 1972

Faith in America

There are many who feel "the windows of the world are covered with rain"[16] —that our future is gloomy and difficult to change. But if we are without hope we will do little to overcome the obstacles in our path. We must go forward with faith in God and faith in our country.

At this time of year, we honor two of America's greatest leaders—George Washington and Abraham Lincoln. If ever there were two men who had a right to doubt the future of our country it was these two American presidents: Washington as he led his country in its struggle for birth, and Lincoln as he struggled for its survival. Yet both men emerged from their dark days of tenure as America's most respected leaders.

George Washington's advice to his fellow countrymen still applies to present generations. "Let us raise a standard to which the wise and honest can repair," he said, "the event is in the hands of God."[18] If Washington and his colleagues did indeed raise the proper standards at the Constitutional Convention, then it is our responsibility to be honest enough to keep them in repair, and wise enough to seek the help of God.

Washington also said that "Few men have virtue to withstand the highest bidder."[18] There are many today who bid for our attention in an effort to convince us that this country, with its time-proven, God-given system of government, is about to collapse. But it will not happen —not if we maintain our faith in God and country.

Even in the darkest hour of April 1865, when James Garfield stood on a balcony in New York City and declared that President Lincoln was dead, our nation remained whole. Lincoln was dead, but, as Garfield said, "God reigns and the Government at Washington lives."[19]

99

What we need today is for each of us to believe, as did Washington and Lincoln, in the United States of America as a Government of the people, by the people, and for the people.

More than five decades ago, another U.S. President made a comment which was prophetic and worth repeating. "America's present need," he said, "is not heroics but healing; not nostrums but normalcy; not revolution but restoration...."[20]

What we need is faith in America.

FEBRUARY 17, 1974

10

THE PROMISE OF THE FUTURE

eternal life | future | the purpose of life

and eternal progression

*To know one's purpose in life
includes knowing that we are children
of a living Father in heaven
with whom we once dwelt
before coming to earth.
It also means
knowing that we are here to learn,
progress, and be tested
in order that we
might prove
our worthiness to
return to the presence of
our Father in heaven.*

The Promise of the Future

We spend a great deal of our lifetime worrying about the possibility of old things being "done away." Rightfully, we want to keep things that are of value to us as long as we can, but sometimes our fear of losing them robs us of our enjoyment of them.

We have probably all seen individuals with new furniture, new cars or new clothes who refuse to use them because they are afraid of wearing them out. Their fear is not only focused on the possible loss of familiar possessions, but that they won't become new again. A similar situation often exists in our personal relationships with loved ones.

Life is an on-going process. It began before we were born; it will continue after we die. In a word, it is eternal. But sometimes we become so attached to the present that we become fearful of the future. Understandably, we would all like to stop life at its most pleasant moment, to cherish and live that happiness forever. But that is not the purpose of life—only the promise of the future. The danger is in allowing this natural desire to become an interfering obsession, to let it distort our vision.

Life is intended to be lived. It is a learning and training experience which prepares us for a better life—a plan which calls for all things to be "done away," so that all can become new. If we fail to understand that basic premise, then today's happiness can truly become tomorrow's burden. That is what often happens when parents become overprotective and try to spare a child the experiences of life for fear that life will rob them of the child. It happens when a partner in marriage becomes so jealous that love turns to distrust. And it also happens when we let the passing of a loved one—or even the fear of it—make us bitter toward life.

Yes, the gift of love runs deep just as God intended. It is one of the few things that lasts beyond this mortal existence. It is eternal, like life itself. Little wonder then that we cling to cherished moments and are saddened at the loss of those we love. But it should be only a temporary sorrow, softened with the understanding that love and family relationships are as permanent as we want them.

Much remains to be known about the life to come, but of this we can be sure—it will come, and with it the promise of the future.   MAY 25, 1975

Sometime We'll Understand

A great American pioneer once said, "We shall never see the time when we shall not need to be taught."[1] Learning and growing is a basic part of life, and to progress is the very reason for our existence here upon earth. But with our learning we must also obtain understanding. As Solomon was counseled by his father, "Wisdom is the principal thing; therefore get wisdom: and with all thy getting get understanding."[2]

Understanding is often difficult, but without it knowledge can be a dangerous thing. As one wise man recently remarked, "Some of our...students...apparently haven't learned that their little learning was not a dangerous thing if they realized that what they knew was only a little learning."[3]

We live in a time of great scientific discovery and advancement, a time which requires much understanding. And part of the understanding which is required of us is the realization that God controls the amount of knowledge man receives. It is more than coincidental that the human race had made little or no progress for thousands of years, and then, within just the past century, has made strides even our wisest forefathers would find difficult to comprehend. Understanding that our discoveries are controlled by the hand of God is as important as knowledge itself.

103

It is also important to know there are some things we might not be permitted to understand. "God [does move] in a mysterious way His wonders to perform."[4] Have we not all experienced tragedy and heartache and asked ourselves why? Who is there who has not prayed and seemingly received no answer? And who has not looked into the heavens and wondered how it was all possible? One of the most comforting perceptions we may have is to know that we may not be permitted to understand all things now, but that all answers will be revealed in time.

Maxwell Cornelius expressed it best in these words put to song by James McGranahan:

"Not now, but in the coming years,...We'll read the meaning of our tears,...We'll catch the broken threads again and finish what we here began; Heaven will the mysteries explain, And then, ah, then we'll understand."[5]

And so it is with all our learning, which is great and good, we also need understanding—the most important being a trust in God and to know that "sometime, sometime we'll understand."[5]   OCTOBER 15, 1972

The Purpose of Life

We are all indebted to the pioneers in every age and every generation. They are the stouthearted, fearless individuals with the faith to blaze new trails and challenge impossible dreams. Indeed, we owe much to those who came before us.

The settlers who led the Western movement in the last century—they who are traditionally known as "pioneers"—probably exemplify the qualities of pioneering more than any other single group. They had many attributes, but one characteristic stood out: They seemed to know and understand their purpose in life. And its importance is as great to us in the present as it was to those pioneers of the past.

Recently it was asked, "What is the most important thing we should learn?" And the answer given was "To know one's purpose in life." That includes knowing that we are children of a living Father in heaven with whom we once dwelt before coming to earth. It also means knowing that we are here to learn, progress, and be tested in order that we might prove our worthiness to return to the presence of our Father in heaven. And it would be well to have an understanding of "life after death" and its special challenges and rewards for us.

As we become acquainted with the spiritual guideposts of life it is also important for us to know the meaning of work and the satisfaction that comes from honest labor. And we need to develop a true love for our fellowman and respect him for what he is and for what he does.

Such is the purpose of life, and it appears to be William Clayton's message in the following hymn which he wrote while traveling West with the pioneers more than a century ago.

> *Come, come, ye saints,*
> *no toil nor labor fear;*
> *But with joy wend your way....*
>
> *Why should we mourn*
> *or think our lot is hard?*
> *'Tis not so; all is right....*
>
> *We'll find the place*
> *which God for us prepared,...*
> *And should we die*
> *before our journey's through,*
> *Happy day! all is well!*
> *All is well!*[6]

JULY 22, 1973

105

"...To stand and stare"

If there is any place the "glory of the Lord" is revealed "that all flesh can see it together,"[7] it is in the heavens. On this subject Lincoln also added, "...I cannot conceive how [man] could look up into the heavens and say there is no God."[8]

Perhaps our challenge is to take the time to look. The poet William Henry Davies wrote, "What is this life if, full of care,/We have no time to stand and stare?"/[9] But too often in our hustle-bustle world we do not take the time to really observe anything, and so the dimensions of our lives shrink and our spiritual awareness begins to suffer.

One might well ask, just what should we look at? And perhaps the answer is "anything." But let us suggest a few ideas that could add to our spiritual insights.

The Psalmist wrote, "The heavens declare the glory of God; and the firmament sheweth his handiwork."[10] But, unfortunately, in our urbanized city life, we not only seldom look heavenward, we sometimes, in fact, forget the stars are even there. And when we do glance upward it is usually the handiwork of man we see rather than the natural wonder of the works of God.

The joys of nature also offer a multitude of spiritual uplifts if we will but make the effort to look for them. He who has not experienced the simple communion with nature has missed one of life's greatest joys. Through the eyes of a child we may see again the loveliness of things we have forgotten or have taken for granted. We can observe the incredible engineering feats of the termite building his towering home—equivalent to a human milehigh apartment building, or the nest of the weaverbird, delicately woven and fastened with knots a Boy Scout has to learn. And the work of the bee! Engineers and computers have been unable to design a more efficient use of space than the hexagonal cell of the bee which uses only one and one-half ounces of wax to hold four pounds of honey.

And if we truly want to reflect on life, we should simply stand and stare at a newborn infant. It is then that we find the answer to the Psalmist's question, "What is man, that thou art mindful of him?"[11] For surely through the miracle of creation we are reminded of the eternal nature of our own spirit.

Yes, it is often difficult to maintain our perspective in a world that seems to be rushing by us. But if we will occasionally take a moment to observe the wondrous things around us, perhaps we will better understand the miracle of our own existence, and offer our praise to the Lord.

MARCH 16, 1975

They Live Forevermore

Every person who has lost someone close to them, and I suppose that includes nearly all of us, knows the heartache that comes from the death of a loved one. Such sorrow apparently was felt by Stephen Foster when he wrote "Gentle Annie." And such feelings seem to have prompted him to ask, "Thou art gone...Annie...Shall we nevermore behold thee, never hear thy...voice again?"[12]

To that question and to all who wonder if there is life after death, we offer today our firm conviction that there is. Life does go on. It continues forever!

How sad it is for those who believe that life ends at the grave. Gratefully that isn't so. There is no greater joy and inner peace than that which comes from a firm belief, even to the point of knowledge, that life is eternal.

As we honor those who have left us—whether they be fallen battlefield heroes, victims of accident or

107

illness, or simply those who have completed their earthly stay—we must remember with assurance that they do live on.

The sorrow we feel should not be for them, nor for what they are missing, but rather for ourselves and our temporary separation from them. And then, in another way, we should feel a certain happiness instead of sadness —happiness because we knew them, and because, hopefully, we will find joy in recalling the choice and pleasant experiences that linger in our memories. But most important, happiness in the knowledge that someday we will renew our old acquaintances.

As G. S. Merriam once said, "...to us here, death is the most terrible word we know. But when we have tasted its reality, it will mean to us birth, deliverance, a new creation of ourselves."[13]

In the words of the song: "Their bodies are buried in peace, but their name," and we would add their souls, "liveth evermore."[14]   MAY 28, 1972

11

THE DEVELOPMENT OF CHARACTER

character | reputation | greed

temper | violence | virtue

chastity | morality

temptation and hostility

*Our character is what
distinguishes us from others.
It is the way we think
and act when no one is looking,
when we are sure no one
will ever find out what we have done.
It is what we really are, not
what others think we are.*

109

The Development of Character

What we have or what we do in life is not nearly so important as what we are: for what we are is the sum of our character, and it is our character which gives our lives meaning.

Good character cannot be purchased, borrowed, or given away. It must be built slowly and carefully, not in an hour or a day, but during the course of a lifetime. Author Maltbie Babcock wrote, "The workshop of character is everyday life. The uneventful and commonplace hour is where the battle is lost or won."[1]

And we do not fight that battle alone. Many influence the development of our character. Although parents cannot deliver character to us in a package, they are responsible for the traits and attributes which make us what we are. We learn love from those who love us; charity from the charitable; faith from trial and hardship; and courage from endurance and defeat. And the opposite is just as true: If hate is all we see then we cannot be expected to know love. We learn slowly and silently, and usually from others.

Good character does not appear spontaneously. It is developed through life and living—through exposure to light and darkness. A photograph is a good analogy—too much light and the picture is void of detail; too little light and the picture is left in darkness. And so it is with life—it takes the right amount of teaching, example and experience to build good character, and usually it evolves so slowly we fail to see when we are getting the wrong amount of "light"—when our character is poorly nourished with too much of what is bad for us or too little of what is right.

As we have said before, it was Brooke Westcott who said we grow weak or strong "Silently and imperceptibly as we wake or sleep,...and at last some crisis shows us for what we have become."[2]

It is, therefore, incumbent upon each of us to make a conscious effort to fill our lives with the kind of experiences—the right kind of experiences—which will help us develop good character. AUGUST 5, 1973

Character Is What We Really Are

Our character is what distinguishes us from others. It is the way we think and act when no one is looking, when we are sure no one will ever find out what we have done. It is what we *really* are, not what others *think* we are.

Character doesn't come by chance; it takes time and patience to develop. It is earned through experience of trial and suffering; it is built by overcoming weaknesses. We build character when we conquer an undesirable passion, thought, or desire. Trifling though it may seem, it becomes another mark on our character.

A man is literally what he thinks, his character being the complete sum of all his thoughts and feelings. Man is the molder of his own character; it is made or unmade by himself.

Character is not to be confused with reputation. "A man's character is the reality of himself," said Henry Ward Beecher. "His reputation is the opinion others have formed of him."[3]

William Davis observed the difference this way:

> *The circumstances amid which you live determine your reputation; the truth you believe determines your character.*
>
> *Reputation is what you are supposed to be; character is what you are...*
>
> *Reputation is what you have when you come to a new community; character is what you have when you go away....*

Reputation is made in a moment; character is built in a lifetime....
Reputation makes you rich or makes you poor; character makes you happy or makes you miserable.
Reputation is what men say about you on your tombstone; character is what angels say about you before... God. [4]

It is true that a good reputation is important, but it is meaningful only when backed by an equally good character. "A good name is seldom regained," wrote Joel Hawes. "When character is gone, all is gone, and one of the richest jewels of life is lost forever." [5]   SEPTEMBER 24, 1972

The Aspect of Greed

We once quoted a verse which read, "For it must needs be, that there is opposition in all things....the one being sweet and the other bitter." [6] Indeed, life is paradoxical. "Without evil, there would be no good; without darkness, there would be no light;...[and] without the valleys, there would be no mountains." [7]

Today we would apply this same concept to our individual lives. President Gus Turbeville of South Carolina's Coker College recently welcomed students by pointing out that without others we would have no self-concept. "Without a sense of self," he said, "you could not be... good, generous, kind and considerate,...Life is a constant battle between the good and evil aspects of self,..." [7]

One of man's most negative traits—one of the evil aspects of self—is greed. It has taken such a foothold in the lives of so many that it "is almost a way of life in the world today,...There is no question that greed is a major factor in our alarmingly high crime rate, [that it is responsible for the cheating which runs rampant in] our schools, businesses, and government." [7] To continue quoting President Turbeville: "We give a great deal of lip service to law and order, but all too often we obey only those laws we want to or the ones we are afraid we can't successfully evade....

"We get terrified and indignant by the holdup man, the burglar, and the shoplifter. But is a shoplifter any more a thief than a person who knowingly sells shoddy merchandise through misleading advertising? Is a holdup man any more a moral criminal than the physician, lawyer, mechanic, or plumber who overcharges for his services? Is the burglar more of a criminal than the manufacturer who pollutes the air and water in violation of our laws? Is the pickpocket any more a wrongdoer than the professor or the college administrator who gives less than his all to his constituency? Is the truant any more delinquent than the student who wants a degree but not an education?"[7]

Greed is the underlying cause of most of these actions, and could well be the most destructive force in the world today. Silently and imperceptibly, its immoral influence creeps up on us and weakens the very foundation of our character. To fight it is a full-time effort, and a personal battle which can only be waged within one's self.

SEPTEMBER 12, 1973

Temper...Governs the Whole Man

There is in each of us the seed of self-control, the power to be master of our own character, to act according to our own conscience. But there is also a passion which often gets in the way of self-mastery. It is the loss of one's temper, and it has resulted in more tragedy and sorrow than any other human trait. William Jordan said, "The second most deadly instrument of destruction is the gun—the first is the human tongue."[8]

113

We all have tempers. They are a quality of disposition, an integral part of our character. But they must be regulated, because the degree to which we have mastery over ourselves is always measured by how well we control our temper. "Temper, if ungoverned," said Anthony Ashley Cooper, "governs the whole man."[9]

There will always be a need to control our disposition, perhaps more so today because of man's increasing and varied knowledge. We must be tolerant of others. We must not leave our tempers unchecked when there are differences of opinion. Lord Chesterfield wrote, "A man who cannot command his temper should not think of being a man of business."[10] And we could add, a man of politics, or public service, or education as well.

Last week we spoke of courage. There is no doubt that it takes great courage to control one's temper. Many say a quick release of temper is a safety valve for inner tension. But the danger, of course, is the hurt which can be caused in a moment of anger, and the regret which comes when we regain our composure.

Perhaps we should remember the words of the seventeenth-century Spanish philosopher Baltasar Gracian: "Never act in passion. If you do all is lost. You cannot act for yourself if you are not yourself and passion always drives out reason....As soon as you notice that you are losing your temper beat a wise retreat."[11] JUNE 11, 1972

"Thou Shalt Not Kill"

No compassionate, loving person can condone the violence that seems so widespread in the world today. Events at the

114

1972 Olympic games in Munich gained world-wide attention, and quickly brought to mind the troubled conditions which plague our planet.

The earth has seldom been a place of peace and tranquility. History proves it, and there is little reason to believe it will change before the Prince of Peace returns. Most assuredly, the Adversary will continue to influence the souls of men, perhaps with even greater fervor in these latter days.

And so the question might be asked, "What should be our course?" Should we surrender and allow the followers of evil free reign? Quite the contrary. There is an even greater need for those who love life and liberty to be a positive influence in the lives of others. If every human being would keep the simple commandments "Thou shalt not kill" and "Thou shalt not steal," many of the world's problems would disappear. Is it little wonder that one spiritual leader recently commented: "The only way we will solve the problems of the world is through the Gospel of Jesus Christ."[12] He has given us the formula for peace, yet we cannot seem to follow even the simplest part of it.

Some of us may see violence only in other cities and other lands, but it occurs as well in our own neighborhoods and in our own families. We must teach correct principles to those we influence in order that there will be a proper degree of reverence for life in our homes. We cannot expect the world to be any better than the laws we are willing to obey, or the commandments we are willing to keep. And we must not be discouraged. The Lord is willing to help. Our fathers did not give up in the face of difficulty, and we should follow in their footsteps. We should do as they did: acknowledge the hand of God and follow the guideposts He has given—for the day of peace *will* come.

As Theodore Curtis suggested in his verse:

Lean on my ample arm,
Oh, thou depressed!...
If thou wilt come to Me,
Thou shalt have rest.[13]

SEPTEMBER 10, 1972

To Be Free of Violence

Disagreement among people is a common, perhaps even necessary part of our daily existence. But too often we feel that because someone's point of view is different from ours, he is our enemy and must be stopped. As such thoughts grow, disagreement soon turns to violence, and that is a sad comment on life.

During the past decade, violence spurred by a disagreement in political philosophies has resulted in the death of an American president, the death of his brother who was a presidential candidate, the killing of civil rights leaders, and more recently, an attempt on the life of another presidential candidate. All were senseless acts of violence, triggered because someone had a different point of view.

Certainly there will be opposing views. There is nothing wrong with that. As Gandhi said, "It is not our differences that really matter. It is the meanness behind [them] that is ugly."[14]

If we are to be free of violence in our nations and towns, we must also be free of it in our hearts, our homes, our streets and our factories. We cannot settle our differences through violent action and expect happiness to follow. If we disagree with our loved ones or fellow workers, we must try to work out our differences sensibly, or at least allow the other person his point of view.

Granted, that is not an easy course to follow. Self-control now seems to be in limited supply, and a violent

116

response to those who disagree with us is often the easiest and quickest course to follow.

Perhaps we should remember the feelings of King Arthur when he learned that his friend Lancelot had betrayed him. The king knew that to revile against Lancelot would destroy the Camelot he had built and he wisely pointed out that strength is not found in violence, nor weakness in compassion; that through the grace of God they could live through their difficulty together. So must be our understanding, also, if we are to be free of violence.

MAY 21, 1972

A Commitment to Virtue

In the course of history many eras, styles, fads and customs have come and gone. For the most part society has been improved because of them, although occasionally the improvement was due to their leaving rather than their coming.

Today we live in an excessively liberal age of fads and customs unimaginable a decade or two ago, and many people in the world anxiously sense the need to return to a standard, which hopefully, may only have left us momentarily—a commitment to virtue.

Morality is not simply a fad or style. It is a commandment given by our Creator for our happiness and eternal joy. But unfortunately, it is not viewed as such today. Morality is regarded as something old-fashioned, without value to twentieth-century man. Today's call is for a person to do as his mortal appetites dictate, without concern for Diety or the eternal man. The cry is to accept the "new morality" which, as others have said, is nothing more than the old immorality.

Immoral behavior creeps up on us. It is, as one educator stated, "...a special form of insanity. It reflects

117

a kind of blackout in which we either lack or lose perspective about the consequences of our thoughts, words, and actions."[15] Social customs which were totally unacceptable a decade ago are now commonplace; acts which were once scorned and rejected are now accepted. The danger is that many may embrace this behavior simply because we let it become commonplace.

When one speaks of virtue and chastity these days, he is often charged with being narrow-minded or out of touch with reality. Yet, in truth, the reality is that immorality in any form is sin in the eyes of God. A former newspaper editor and church leader once wrote, "[God's] law is irrevocable and inescapable and applies to all, whether we believe in God or not....No amount of rationalizing can change God's law. No amount of fashion designing can turn immodesty into virtue and no amount of popularity can change sin into righteousness."[16] JULY 29, 1973

Avoid Life's Shocking Moments

No doubt we would all like it said of us that he fought the good fight. Ran the straight race.[17] Certainly, most of us try, but perhaps too often we are tempted to give in to what seems to be the easy way.

All of us are influenced by the people and circumstances around us. The fact cannot be changed, but we can control our surroundings to some degree. We can control the atmosphere and type of people with which we become involved. That is where we need to fight the good fight. The kind of entertainment we select, the people we choose to socialize with, and our recreational activities in general, all have a direct influence on who we are and what we stand for.

In these days of great permissiveness, we may wonder what harm could come from seeing a particular movie. But consider this: our minds and our memories—

118

indeed our character—are a reflection of all we have ever seen, heard, thought, or done. Though we may not repeat the actions we've seen on the screen, the idea, particularly a shocking one, will stay with us.

We have all had regretful experiences over which we had no control, experiences now indelibly etched in our memories. Our task is to avoid life's "shocking moments" in which we do have a choice. The base, the sordid, the degrading things we see, even on a movie screen, have a way of becoming a permanent part of our being. As one individual remarked, "You can't order remembrance out of a man's mind."[18] When we see or hear something that is contrary to our character, it seems to stamp that thought forever on our memory. And once there, it lingers to tempt us into witnessing similar events again and again. Gradually, like the erosion of a canyon, our moral fiber is weakened and often destroyed. How much better it would have been had we avoided those influences. It is not always easy, but it is always rewarding.

This, then, is our battleground. Hopefully we will have the strength and courage to make our stand—to "fight the good fight." JUNE 24, 1973

"...Enter Not Into Temptation"

Everyone who passes through the portals of mortal existence suffers the pangs of temptation, Jesus the Christ not excepted. We are all subject to the wiles of Satan. His enticements are manifest in many varieties and disguises, and most of us will confront them sometime in life.

To be tempted is a vital part of God's plan, for without temptation there would be no challenge, no test to determine what is right, no victory over evil. Without such trials there would be no opportunity to prove our worthiness for greater blessings. As one author wrote, "It

119

is good to be without vices, but it is not good to be without temptations."[19] Indeed, mortal life would lose part of its divine purpose if we did not face these challenges.

But realizing that we will be tempted does not mean we should seek temptations. In fact, the opposite holds true—we should do all in our power to avoid them if possible. It was for this reason the Savior advised us to pray, "...lead us not into temptation, but deliver us from evil,..[20]

The best way to avoid succumbing to temptation is to shun it, for one temptation leads to another. There is no way to give in a little. Today's indulgence becomes tomorrow's commonplace and soon we find ourselves doing things we previously thought inconceivable. To resist requires practice and if we don't practice overcoming relatively harmless temptations, we will not have sufficient strength to resist the truly dangerous ones.

And this, too, should be remembered: There is no temptation that cannot be overcome. One ancient prophet wrote, "God...will not suffer you to be tempted above that ye are able; but will with the temptation also make a way to escape, that ye may be able to bear it."[21]

It is not necessary for us to seek temptation—it will find us soon enough. And it usually does when we are most vulnerable. Satan did not tempt Christ to turn the stones to bread immediately following a meal, but waited until Jesus had fasted forty days. So it is with us. There is no temptation unless a desire is aroused within us. The test comes when the desire is great and the flesh is weak. As George Washington remarked, "Few men have virtue enough to withstand the highest bidder."[22]

Temptation will surely come, not just once, but continually; not in a single, grand encounter, but in a persistent barrage throughout life. To avoid it is not always possible, but to resist it is if we follow the words of our Savior to "Watch and pray, that ye enter *not* into temptation."[23]

NOVEMBER 3, 1974

Honesty—Whatever the Temptation

We face no greater challenge in our everyday affairs than that of being honest. Honesty is one of the most refined elements of character and one of the most difficult traits to develop. It is evident in almost everything we do. We cannot answer a question, make a statement, transact the least important of our daily affairs without taking a stand for or against honesty.

No one escapes the temptation to be dishonest, but if we maintain our position for honesty before temptation arrives, we stand a better chance for victory. If we wait until we find some misplaced money to decide how we will react, chances are we will lose our battle for integrity. But if we decide beforehand that we will be honest at all cost, under any circumstance, whatever the temptation: stealing, lying, cheating, immorality—then the conflict is eased. All have their roots in dishonesty.

We must also always conduct our life as if our acts were seen. Even when we are alone, we should live as if the eyes of the world were upon us. As Shakespeare wrote:

> *"This above all: to thine own self be true,*
> *And it must follow, as the night the day,*
> *Thou canst not then be false to any man."*[24]

None of us would willfully teach our children to be dishonest, but that is the principle we teach when we promise to do something and then willfully, purposefully, don't do it, or when we fail to point out a clerk's error after we have received too much change. Honor and honesty are basic to our way of life, for without trust among people there would be no private or public confidence in any relationship.

Who would feel safe with a doctor who had cheated his way through medical school, or a pilot who had lied to get his license? There is no question but what we want everyone we deal with to be honest, and they want nothing less from us.

Yes, the need to be honest confronts each of us every minute of every day. It is important that we be true both to ourselves and to others. It will make our world a better place in which to live; for, at the very least, as Carlyle suggested, when we "Make [ourself] an honest man...then [we] may be sure there is one less rascal in the world."[25]

APRIL 1, 1973

Truthful Memories

The memories we have are forceful reminders of how swiftly the years pass by, how quickly one season follows another, how some days are full of happiness while others are laden with sorrow. Because our days do pass quickly, it is important that we live each one of them fully, meaningfully and honestly.

Honest moments add meaning to life. Dishonest moments almost always take away from life's fullness, and tend to be the moments we look back on with tears, not happiness. And more often than not, they are the moments that began with a simple untruth.

When we lie, we are polluting our spiritual resources just as certainly as we are polluting our physical resources when we carelessly throw trash on the ground. Any pollution is harmful. Any lie is dishonest. There is no such thing as a little lie.

Yet, a recent national article told how our fellow citizens "cover up" questionable activities through the use of so-called "little lies." And the distressing aspect

122

of the article is that it makes such lies sound perfectly common and acceptable. But is it acceptable when an employee feigns an illness because he wants to take the day off? Or a student makes up a story to avoid an exam? Is it acceptable when an advertiser admittedly exaggerates his product to make it appear better? When a reporter knowingly covers up important facts, or a public servant writes false and misleading reports?

When these things happen—and they do—there is little wonder that politicians fall into traps such as the one known as "Watergate."

Perhaps if any good is to come from the events of the past few months in Washington, it is the stark reminder to us all to return to honesty. Truthfulness is not a quality we can use one day and discard the next. Truthfulness must be constant and become a part of our lives—always. And if it is, it can improve the quality of life for everyone.

Yes, an honest life passes just as quickly as a dishonest one, but the sunrises and sunsets of truthful memories are more likely to be laden with happiness than with tears.

JANUARY 27, 1974

12

TO
KNOW
YOURSELF

inner self | self-love, self-reliance

self-esteem

self-communication and self-control

This above all, to thine own self be true.
WILLIAM SHAKESPEARE

To Know Yourself

As we go about this business of living, our character is continually being evaluated by those around us. Such is inevitable, for although we have been taught to "Judge not, that ye be not judged,"[1] we still cannot help but make value judgments about those with whom we associate.

There is a need for presentable behavior at all times but it should be in harmony with our inner self. We are untrue to ourselves and others if we assume a facade and pretend to be something we are not. If change is required, then change is what we should do, for our best side should be our only side.

If we really want to know ourselves, to know what we really are like, we should conduct a critical self-examination during moments of stress. Our true character is more likely to emerge when we are under pressure than when we are in complete control and all is going well.

For this reason we can probably learn more about a man during the tense moments of a hard-fought ball game than we can during a serene Sunday morning in church. That is not to say we should play ball instead of attending worship services. Quite the contrary; for the principles of character we learn in church are an integral part of our total development. The point is that what we are is what we do at *all* times—not just at moments of our own choosing.

Bishop Brooke Foss Westcott of England put it this way: "Great occasions do not make heroes or cowards, they simply unveil them in the eyes of man. Silently and imperceptibly as we wake or sleep we grow strong or weak, and at last some crisis shows us for what we have become."[2]

Henri Amiel once observed that "the worth of a man" is not revealed by "what he has," or does, but by

125

"what he is."[3] And what we are cannot be turned on and off at will. It is a part of us, deep within, and it surfaces in every circumstance. Our challenge, therefore, is to so live every day that what we are, is, in truth, what we would like to be.   MAY 6, 1973

Seven Simple Words

For years we have indulged ourselves in the belief that all our problems could be solved by the sciences. We have deluded ourselves with the idea that more knowledge, more technology and more science would provide the answers. But as valuable as knowledge and science are, they have not changed the nature of our problems, for many of them lie within the hearts of men—problems of human conduct and social behavior.

Although these difficulties come to us in modern dress, they are the same old problems that have always plagued mankind: greed, lust, desire for dominion over others, self-righteousness.

If we are to have a better society, it will not be assembled in think-tanks or by computers. It will be fashioned in the hearts of man. It will be found in seven simple words given long ago, "...thou shalt love thy neighbor as *thyself:*..."[4] This commandment is the core of proper human conduct, and all the sciences cannot reduce its potential impact.

How simple the lesson if we could but learn it! Seven words, which, if properly applied, could remove most of the anguish from the conduct of human affairs.

But why is the lesson so hard to learn? Perhaps because we look outside ourselves for the answers instead of first looking into our own hearts. If we would begin to change the world, we must begin with ourselves—and that is also where true happiness can be found.

126

Perhaps the difficulty of this great lesson is its simplicity. "...thou shalt love thy neighbor as thyself:..." This message is self-evident and easily understood, but to follow the advice is the challenge.   MAY 18, 1975

Power Over Ourselves

There is a quote from Seneca which says, "Most powerful is he who has himself in his power."[5] Indeed, self-control is one of our greatest challenges and the gateway to our greatest opportunities.

"Man has two creators," said William George Jordan, "his god and himself. His first creator furnishes him the raw material of his life...[but] it is what man makes of himself that counts."[6]

Nearly everyone knows right from wrong, but not everyone does what is right. As a friend of mine recently said, "Wouldn't it be easy if we could only do what we know we are supposed to do?" That is a product of self-discipline and self-control, and John Locke describes it as "The most precious of all [our] possessions...."[7]

Developing self-control is one of the severest tests we face. At each moment of our life we are either king or slave to ourselves. As we surrender to a wrong appetite, or to any human weakness or failure, we are a slave; but as we master those wrongs or weaknesses, we create a new self and rule our lives with strength and wisdom. Self-mastery gives us the power to follow our convictions, and to better withstand the trials of life we are sure to face.

So often we are tempted to do things because they appear pleasurable, or because we find it difficult to say no, but Aristotle reminds us that "What it lies in our power to do, it lies in our power not to do."[8] False pleasure can quickly turn to pain, and we not only hurt ourselves but

127

those around us as well. The secret to mental and spiritual health is self-mastery. It permits us to rule both our pleasure and our pain.

We can all gain self-control if we are willing to pay the price. The payments are small expenditures of mental, physical and moral energy; and the return is new inner strength and power in times of need. It has been said that self-control can be developed through small daily exercises in moral gymnastics: 1) Put down an interesting book at the most thrilling page. 2) Jump out of bed at the first moment's waking. 3) Walk a short distance when a ride is offered.[9]

Such simple exercises in self-discipline will have a wondrous effect on our whole moral nature, and will help us develop "The most precious of all [our] possessions,... [the] power over ourselves."[7]

OCTOBER 22, 1972

The Security of Self-Reliance

Perhaps the most valuable result of all education is self-reliance, the ability to make ourselves do the things we know must be done, whether we like it or not. Not only is it one of the most valuable lessons we learn, it is also one of the most difficult.

Self-reliance is at the core of all individual progress. But often we fail many times before we begin to believe in our own thoughts, before we begin to think and act for ourselves and come to understand that personal success depends upon a reliance on one's own efforts and abilities. Psychologists have stated that unhappiness, loneliness, crime and similar distresses arise directly from a lack of emotional and physical self-reliance. The extent to which we are able to rely on our own inward abilities is directly related to success in life. And it is the quiet, internal security of self-trust that helps us most when the going gets rough.

It is easy to decide what is good and true, from the security and solitude of our own homes. But our principles and beliefs are often challenged when we encounter the buffetings of the outside world. It is then that self-convictions are most needed, for without them there is a tendency to disregard our own best impulses when we are in the company of others.

Unfortunately, the sad chain of events does not end there. For as we begin to compromise with duty and integrity, our self-esteem begins to crumble. Our initiative falters. And the quiet decay of self-reliance is set in motion.

Self-confidence is the foundation of self-trust. As Vashnie Young said, "There is no finer sensation in life than that which comes with victory over one's self. It feels good to be fronting into a hard wind, winning against its power, but it feels a thousand times better to go forward to a goal of inward achievement, brushing aside all your old internal enemies as you advance."[10]

Emerson said to "Trust thyself...if we live truly, we shall see truly."[11] And as we learn to know and master ourselves, each conquest over weakness—no matter how small—will give us renewed courage and build our self-reliance for the time we need it most.   MARCH 9, 1975

On Knowing Ourself

We spend all of our life learning—not just the traditional kind of education, but learning about people, about places, and about things around us. All of it is important, indeed, it is one of the purposes of life itself. But it is vital that we not neglect another important part of education—learning about ourselves. Unless we know ourselves, we cannot know others, or God. Self-knowledge is paramount in understanding all other knowledge.

A seventeenth-century Spanish philosopher said, "You cannot master yourself unless you know yourself. There are mirrors for the face but none for the mind. Let careful thought about yourself serve as a substitute."[12]

There are many aspects of self-knowledge: What makes us sad or happy? How well do we face sorrow? Do we let discouragement turn into defeat? When are we honest, humble and charitable—and for what reasons? Is our success true accomplishment or just boastful pride? Does our love come from the heart? These are some of the questions we must answer in order to develop a better understanding of ourselves.

Another important part of self-knowledge is knowing our temptations—the boundaries within which we should operate. One author wrote, "If a man does not know what are his greatest temptations, he must have been a stranger indeed to the business of self-examination."[13] A painter does not begin his work of art until he has determined the size of his canvas. How much more important it is that we determine our own limits as we work toward the fulfillment of our lives.

The enemy of mankind takes care to subtly draw us into sin, usually by gradually enticing us into degrees of temptation. As sin is disguised, so is temptation, and if we are to know ourselves thoroughly, we must be aware of the temptations to which we are most vulnerable.

Temptations or ideas, as one has suggested, "resemble fine sand thrown upon the surface of water; it floats for a little while, then sinks…and forms a layer at the bottom."[13] So it is with the temptations which face us daily. However simple they may be, they remain for a while at the surface of our understanding, and unless we recognize them and clear them away, they will sink and form a thick deposit on our conscience and moral personality.

And finally, self-knowledge requires self-honesty. As Polonius advised his son in Shakespeare's *Hamlet,* "This above all: to thine own self be true,..."[14]   NOVEMBER 4, 1973

"...*Love...Thyself*"

"Thou shalt love they neighbour as thyself." So spoke the Savior when asked by the Pharisee, "...which *is* the great commandment...?" The first, He said, is to love God with all our heart, mind and soul. "...the second," He added, "is like unto it. Thou shalt love thy neighbour as thyself."[15]

When we review this commandment, we can see the emphasis is on the words "love" and "neighbor," for it is our need to love one another that surely prompted the Savior's remark. But the statement presupposes a condition that we often overlook—that we love ourselves as well.

When we speak of self-love, conceit and selfishness usually come to mind—the very opposite of what the Savior seemed to be saying. But upon closer examination, it is evident that we will not love others unless we love and respect ourselves. That is not conceit. That is simply a humble recognition that we are a child of God; that life has purpose and meaning. We cannot think highly of others unless we think highly of ourselves; therefore, the prerequisite—to love ourselves—before we can truly love others.

A modern-day philosopher has said, "The remarkable thing is that we really [do] love our neighbor as ourselves: we do unto others as we do unto ourselves. We hate others when we hate ourselves. We are tolerant toward others when we tolerate ourselves."[16]

If we have no concern for our own welfare, there is little likelihood that we will have concern for the welfare of others. If we abuse our bodies, we will probably encourage others to do the same. If we see no beauty in nature, it is doubtful we will see any in people; and if we have no love for ourselves, we will find it difficult to feel compassion for our neighbor.

Psychoanalyst David Seabury has suggested that one of our basic laws should be never to compromise ourselves. "No matter what the situation," he said, "[or] how pressing the problem, never give up your integrity. When you do, you make more sorrow than when you don't, hurting everyone in the end."[17] Perhaps we occasionally do things we know we shouldn't because we believe we are doing what others want us to do. But if our actions hurt us, they will eventually hurt others also.

Self-esteem is vital for our success in life. It requires a humble awareness of who we are and why we are here, in order that we might fulfill the commandment to "love thy neighbour as thyself."   SEPTEMBER 22, 1974

Cultivating Our Inner Space

The balm of Gilead is a substance obtained from the sap of a small evergreen tree, with aromatic branches that supposedly soothed and healed. As the song says,[18] the healing was not always of the body, but of the "sin-sick soul" as well.

All our souls need a touch of the balm of Gilead in today's fast-paced world—a soothing balm, a calm comfort which comes from within.

If man's greatest achievement during the past decade were singled out, it would probably be the exploration of outer space. But what about man's inner space—the seat of his intellect, the center of his soul and emotions? There is an even greater need to develop this area.

Too often we are so concerned with our physical body and its needs that we forget to care for the inner self. As one book of spiritual guidance says, "Therefore, care not for the body,...but care for the soul, and for the life of the soul."[19] And as the Savior said, "For what is a man profited, if he shall gain the whole world, and lose his own soul?"[20]

We must learn how to simplify our lives, to slow down, to handle our problems one at a time and not become overburdened with the difficulties of life. We must also develop the ability to be alone with ourselves and our thoughts. Often we head for the country when we want to be alone; yet we have within us the power to retreat into ourselves, and there, if we have cultivated our inner space, we can find immediate tranquility.

Cultivating our inner space should be a key priority in our lives. The benefits are many. Some physicians have observed that a person with good inner capacities is apt to age at a slower rate than an individual without such qualities. Our character is strengthened and improved, and statistics show that men of good character are usually more successful than those with higher intelligence but less firm and integrated characters. Peace of mind is another of the great blessings that comes to one with well-developed inner space. And there are more rewarding associations with others, more enjoyment in the work we do, and greater strength to carry on through difficulties.

The challenge to develop our inner self awaits each of us, and if we accept that challenge, we will also develope within ourselves a soothing restorative balm—a balm to heal the "sin-sick soul." SEPTEMBER 17, 1972

133

On Self-Esteem

We have often discussed the value of introspection—the importance of knowing one's inner self, of respecting and loving oneself. Today we would focus on yet another requirement for mental well-being—the need for self-esteem.

Self-esteem is the regard we have for our own standing or position in life. As children of our Father in heaven, and with spirits as eternal as our Creator's, we have a special responsibility to maintain our self-esteem.

Psychologist Nathaniel Branden believes "there is no value-judgment more important to man, no factor more decisive in his psychological development and motivation, than the estimate he passes on himself."[21]

We are always rationalizing and evaluating our own thoughts and actions. It is a natural, constant part of life. And like everything else we do, it can be good or bad, creative or destructive. But if self-esteem is going to benefit us, then our self-evaluation must be of a positive nature.

We need self-esteem to make proper value judgments, for what we think of ourselves is in large measure responsible for what we do for ourselves. If we are going to achieve true happiness and success, we must respect ourselves and believe we are indeed worthy to enjoy life.

We must also be careful not to let our emotions interfere with our reasoning powers. Psychologist Branden points out that "the ability to distinguish between knowledge and feelings is an essential element in the process of a mind's healthy maturation. It is vital for the achievement and preservation of self-esteem"[21]

It is also important that we recognize the role we can play in helping others build their self-esteem. Nothing will help us believe in ourselves faster than the knowledge that someone else holds us in high regard. We recently mentioned the need we have to be needed, and part of the reason is the self-esteem it builds.

Yes, one of the greatest adventures in living is to get to know ourselves better. We must take time to make friends with ourselves, and we must begin believing in our own talents and special capabilities.

As the great English writer Aldous Huxley once wrote, "There's only one corner of the Universe you can be certain of improving; and that's your own self."[22] If we do this, we will surely build our self-esteem.   OCTOBER 13, 1974

We Are Individually Unique

Part of the masterful plan of creation is that no two people are exactly alike. As Ugo Beggi said, "[We are each]...a thing absolutely unique, not to be confused with any other."[23] For that we should be grateful, for individuality is a part of our free agency—it gives us the opportunity to choose and decide for ourselves what we will be and what we will do. Some choose wisely, and others choose foolishly. But the choice of which road to follow throughout life is ours, and we make our decisions according to our own individual characters and personalities.

One influence that will affect our decisions is the environment which surrounds us and the experiences and circumstances we draw from. Hopefully our inner barometers are calibrated from the righteous teachings of parents and the positive influence of friends and leaders. But if it is out of adjustment, we may find our individuality fading. We may, perhaps even unknowingly, begin to follow the crowd.

Unfortunately, we often take our readings according to worldly standards and measure our success according to how much money we earn, the number of possessions we have, the size of our homes, or the cut of our clothes. Yet, in reality, these superficial values belong to the crowd. They leave little room for individual growth

135

and seldom bring inner peace. We should remember the maxim from Aesop that "Outside show is a poor excuse for inner worth."[24]

Still other aspects of individuality are our talents and abilities. Some people have more talent, some less; some have aptitude in one area, some in another; and some choose to develop their abilities while others do not. Although these choices are part of our free agency, we must also remember that the more we try to develop our skills the stronger and more unique we will become. It was the Savior who emphasized the importance of individual initiative in his parable of the talents. Remember, it was only when the servant sought to develop his talents that he increased his potential.

Finally this thought—individual uniqueness should begin with personal honesty—honesty about who we are and what we will be. And so as we strive for this valuable attribute, perhaps we should remember the wise counsel a father once gave his son: "This above all, to thine own self be true,..."[25]

FEBRUARY 23, 1975

Self-Communication

One of the most talked about phenomenons in this modern age is the miracle of communication. Its potential is almost beyond comprehension, and its need is increasingly important to mankind. But how often do we neglect communicating with ourselves?

Every student knows the value of taking notes, but unfortunately many of us soon forget the importance of a simple pad and pencil.

"Write it down" is not idle, irrelevant advice intended only for those in school. It is a habit most of us could well afford to develop. As one eminent scientist wrote, "There is a limit to how much you can burden your memory; and trying to remember too many things is certainly one of the major sources of psychologic stress."[26] But in addition to stress, we increase the odds of overloading our memory banks, of smothering important data with trivialities that could be recorded on paper. Written reminders to ourselves can eliminate embarrassment, hours of wasted time, and the loss of countless ideas.

Another value in writing our thoughts is expressed in the words of a novelist who recently said that the only reason a writer writes is to find out what he is thinking. Perhaps those of us who have allowed our note-taking skills to grow rusty are missing an unusual opportunity for self-examination. How often do we clarify and critically react to an idea by putting it on paper?

And what about anger and other emotions? Put an angry response on paper, let it cool overnight and you will find that a moment's heated impulse can be transformed into new perspectives and can often save a valuable human relationship in the process.

Family records and diaries are other types of note-taking—forms of self-communication that let us look into the past and develop a working base for the future. Think how indebted we are to the note-takers of history, and what might have been lost had they not been willing to write down what they saw or heard. It was note-taking by the prophets and disciples of Christ that gave us the Bible.

Every mode of communication has its place, and the technical advances achieved by man are needed and valuable. But in our quest for self-improvement and efficiency, there are few of us who would not find life somewhat smoother if we could remember to communicate with ourselves by "writing it down."   FEBRUARY 4, 1973

137

We Are What We Think

The words of Emerson[27] suggest there is something stronger than material force—something more than just what we can see and feel and smell and touch. Thoughts rule the world, indeed, mankind. "We are what we think," is a common saying. Thoughts, it seems, are the starting place for all that ever has been.

Did not the Creator make the mind the most complex and intricate part of this amazing machine we call a body? In fact, so complex is the mind that it alone can control the rest of the human soul—even to the degree of eliminating pain, causing illness, telling us things are true when they are not—even to the point where we believe them.

"As [a man]...thinketh,...so is he,"[28] say the scriptures. Why, then, let ourselves be dragged down by thinking degrading thoughts? "Think on pleasant things," said one. "Deliberately turn your thoughts to something pleasant when the pressures are too tense. And, be careful, as undisciplined thought quickly sifts back to the unhappy, unsettled mind."[29]

George Bernard Shaw said, "...a pessimist is a man who thinks everybody as nasty as himself..."[30] Cannot the opposite be true—an optimist is a man who thinks everybody as happy as himself? Imperfect thoughts, like unsavory characters, can come to anyone's door; but we don't have to let them in. How much better it is to have pleasant, loving, wholesome, productive thoughts.

"Habit is a cable," said Horace Mann. "We weave a thread of it every day, and at last we cannot break it."[31] Should we not begin today to weave a habit of thinking good thoughts, of keeping our minds clear of thoughts that will pull us down to depths of despair? If we think a good thought now, next time it will be that much easier. If we are to become honest, pure, lovely, virtuous and praise-worthy, then we must—as Paul wrote—"think on these things."[32]

FEBRUARY 27, 1972

13

QUALITIES
OF
LEADERSHIP

leadership | principles | conviction

humility | courage | forgiveness

calmness and example

The great men in history
are those who have seemingly
stood alone in defense of their principles.
Their calm courage
came from the peace of mind
that grew from their
unswerving defense of
that which they believed.

140

Qualities of Leadership

Recently we discussed the defeats and setbacks of successful men, and how they used their failures to develop courage and character.

The ability to lead is another characteristic which marks great men. It has been aptly said that "leadership is a 'marriage of situation and personality,' a coming together of the man, the times and the need."[1] The leader sets higher standards for himself than what are merely acceptable. He possesses a sort of energy of will.

Among leaders there is a willingness to respond to new challenges in new ways. Innovation requires courage, and leadership is always strongly linked with courage: the courage to be different, the courage to be wrong or unpopular. It is easy to be safe, to follow the road beaten down by others; but what splendid thing was ever achieved by a concern to be safe or popular?

One of the sadder aspects of contemporary life is that this is the time of the anti-hero. Popular culture tends not only to be preoccupied with what is ordinary; it tends to sneer at what is exceptional or noble. Yet surely we need the hero because he reminds us of the gap between our actual performance and our potential.

Most great leaders have also developed an uncanny ability to sense when the gap between them and those following is too large. As Georg Brandes observed, "The crowd will follow a leader who marches twenty steps in advance, but if he is a thousand steps in front of them, they do not see and do not follow him...."[2]

Great men seem to have a clear vision of what needs to be done and the moral commitment to do it. They do not shrink from the uncomfortable or the unfamiliar or the unwelcome.

141

And probably the most common characteristic of great leadership is the subjection and discipline of the self to larger goals—the recognition of forces within and the imperatives without—which are larger than self. It may be love of country, or of mankind, or of God, as expressed in a stained-glass window of a private chapel for congressmen in the nation's capital. The scene is of George Washington, praying, with the words of the Psalmist: "Preserve me, O God: for in thee do I put my trust."[3]   FEBRUARY 16, 1975

The Defense of Principles

One of the most difficult tests we will ever face in life will be in defense of our convictions. To believe or support an ideal, tenet or philosophy requires thought, judgment and, hopefully, prayer. But to stand firm in that belief—even at the risk of one's life—requires a testimony built of sound conscience and inner strength.

A good conscience is one of the spiritual rewards of righteous living. It is the still, small voice which tells us which precepts are right, which ones we should follow. It gives us confidence and inner tranquility.

In his essay on *Self-Reliance*, Emerson remarked, "Nothing can bring you peace but the triumph of principles."[4] But "Many men do not allow their principles to take root," said Longfellow, "but pull them up every now and then, as children do the flowers they have planted, to see if they are growing."[5]

The great men in history are those who have seemingly stood alone in defense of their principles. Their calm courage came from the peace of mind that grew from their unswerving defense of that which they believed. So it was in the beginning of time, so it was with Christ the Lord, and so it is even today.

142

When Martin Luther stood before the Emperor and was asked to recant what he had written, he said, "I cannot choose but to adhere to the word of God, which has possession of my conscience; nor can I possibly, nor will I ever make any recantation, since it is neither safe nor honest to act contrary to conscience! Here I stand; I cannot do otherwise, so help me God!"[6]

And so should be the firm conviction of us all to the principles which we believe. Hopefully, they will be righteous principles ordained and inspired by the Lord. We may then stand alone. Some may think us wrong, but if our intent is honest and our faith strong, we will walk in serenity with a clear conscience and with the faith that we will never really walk alone.   JANUARY 21, 1973

"Be Thou Humble..."

There are many virtues in life worth striving for and one of the most basic is humility. Confucius said, "Humility is the solid foundation of all virtues."[7] It is a part of one's soul and personality, and often the reason one is loved and desired as a friend and associate. People like to be around those who are humble.

Ironically, the truly humble person is not usually aware that he possesses this important attribute; while others, who recognize its value, sometimes find it a quality which eludes them.

John Ruskin believed that "the first test of a truly great man is his humility."[8] It does not mean one is weak or timid. Quite the opposite. Honest pride and self-respect go hand in hand with the grace of humility. It keeps them in proper perspective.

Humility is also a great equalizer in solving differences of opinion. Nehru once said, "Let us be a little

143

humble;...Let us cooperate with others; let us, even when we do not appreciate what others say, respect their views and their ways of life."[9]

The benefits we derive from humility are sometimes more than we might think. To cite a verse from sacred writings: "Be thou humble; and the Lord thy God shall lead thee by the hand, and give thee answer to thy prayers."[10] What a beautiful and reassuring promise—be humble and the Lord will answer thy prayers!

True success comes through humility, coupled with talent and effort. Often a humble heart can spell the difference between failure and success. There is much wasted talent in many fields of endeavor because others could not see past someone's lack of humility.

And what is the key to humility? A sincere concern for others and the ability to be humble when it is not a necessity. "It is no great thing," wrote St. Bernard, "to be humble when you are brought low; but to be humble when you are praised is a great and rare attainment."[11] Sincerely practiced daily, it will do as much for our lives and the lives of those around us as anything we do, for as Sir John Buchan said, "Without humility there can be no humanity."[12]

AUGUST 13, 1972

It Takes Courage

There is much we do in life that is courageous, even though we may not think so at the time. Courage is a basic human quality. It gives man stability, confidence, a spirit of self-determination.

Unfortunately, many believe this moral fiber is no longer needed, because we have conquered those frightening frontiers of yesterday. But there is a greater need for courage in our lives today than we might suppose. In fact, if we had the courage to live our convictions, many of life's problems would disappear.

It takes courage to admit that one is wrong, and it takes courage to correct the course. For example, there are thousands of alcoholics and drug users who *found* the courage to change, and who now face life without terrifying journeys into oblivion. It was once said, "The glory is not in never failing, but in rising every time you fall."[13]

It takes courage for some parents to sit down with their teenage children and bridge the communications gap between them. Husbands and wives on the brink of divorce need courage to recarve and restructure their marriages— often just the courage to discuss their problems.

And for all of us: It takes courage to get involved in life and the lives of people around us, to help others when they need help, to tolerate differences, to forgive those who have wronged us.

Some may argue, "Yes, it does take courage to do those things, but it's a courage that I don't have." The late President John F. Kennedy pointed out that "To be courageous requires no exceptional qualifications, no magic formula, no special combination of time, place, and circumstance. It is an opportunity that sooner or later is presented to us all...Each man must decide for himself the course he will follow. The stories of past courage can define that ingredient—they can teach, they can offer hope, they can provide inspiration. But they cannot supply courage itself. For this each man must look into his own soul."[14]   JUNE 4, 1972

"To Err Is Human..."

"To err is human, to forgive divine."[15]   There is little doubt about the wisdom of those words, for we all know

145

how easy it is to be in error, and how difficult it is to forgive others for their mistakes. And it is just as difficult to forgive ourselves when we are at fault—or even to admit that we are wrong.

We need not fear making a mistake. The experience can give us new strength and help us grow. Mistakes are inevitable, but we must be sure that we are able and willing to recognize our wrongs when they occur. Admiting our mistakes is usually the most difficult part of the mending process. It is also the most honorable. Yet so often we find ways to excuse our behavior.

An anonymous author has written some humorous comparisons which illustrate how we rationalize our own weaknesses, and often even fail to recognize them:

> *When the other fellow takes a long time to do something, he's slow; but when I take a long time to do something, I'm thorough.*

> *When the other fellow doesn't do it, he's too lazy; but when I don't do it, I'm too busy.*

> *When someone else goes ahead and does something without being told, he's overstepping his bounds; but when I do it, that's initiative.*

> *For one to state his side of a question strongly, is being bullheaded; but for me to do so is being firm.*

> *When the other fellow overlooks a few rules of etiquette, he's rude; but when I skip a few rules, that's originality.*

> *When the other guy makes a mistake, he sure had it coming to him; but for me to make a mistake, WOW, What bad luck.*

> *Funny isn't it—that it is so hard to correct our faults? Maybe it's just because we don't even recognize them—except in others.*

146

To paraphrase Alexander Pope: To err is human —to admit our error is a mark of honesty. SEPTEMBER 16, 1973

Calmness—The Crown of Self-Control

Recently we spoke of the need to step back occasionally from life's busy pace and relax, to take a moment to revitalize ourselves physically, mentally and spiritually.

One of the great benefits of properly pacing our activities is greater serenity and calmness—a calmness which goes beyond relaxation, and affects all we do. It is the cornerstone for happiness and peace of mind. As William George Jordan wrote, "Calmness is the crown of self-control....[It] is the rarest quality in human life."[16]

Calmness is not only an outward sign of character, but a valuable tool for handling our daily affairs. A recently returned prisoner of war said of a fellow POW, "He was always calm, no matter what happened."[17] By remaining unruffled, we are better able to focus on our assignments, maintain self-confidence, adjust to the unexpected, and prevent undue anxiety. It was the Greek philosopher Plato who said, "Nothing in the affairs of men is worthy of great anxiety."[18] And just as anxiety builds from within us, so its antidote comes from within. Serenity and calmness begin at the very depths of our soul.

Perhaps the best time for us to learn the rudiments of calmness is when we are alone. It seems the enemy of calmness is hurry, often brought on by pressure from others. To quote again from William George Jordan, "Hurry is the death blow to calmness,...The words 'Quick Lunches' might properly be placed on thousands of headstones in our cemeteries."[16] Undoubtedly, there are times when haste is needed; but uncontrolled, frantic hurry seldom accomplishes much good.

147

As we have said before, periods of rest and relaxation do not indicate slothfulness. So it is with calmness. The Lord has told us, "Cease to be idle[19]...for he that is idle shall not eat the bread nor wear the garments of the laborer."[20] But at the same time He established for us the pattern, and commanded us to set aside a day of rest, and to work with calm, planned purpose.

Let us then turn to the "God of our fathers, Whose almighty hand" has shown us the way, and let "[His] word [be] our law, [His] paths our chosen way."[21]   MARCH 18, 1973

"Let Your Light So Shine..."

"We are sowing, daily sowing, Countless seeds of good and ill,..."[22] There are few of us who pass through life without affecting—for good or bad—the lives of others, and there is a need for us to be aware of this powerful influence.

Certainly, every parent can agree with the old adage which says one can learn more from a single example than through hours of reading and lecturing. What parents have not had some particular phrase, habit or mannerism return to face them through their children. A simple but wise comment once came from a friend who said, "Don't ever do anything you would not want your son or daughter to do."[23]

Example is contagious, and it is not limited to the home. It is a principle which holds true everywhere. If we work with enthusiasm, we spread the spirit of enthusiasm. On the other hand, if we work with an air of discouragement or indifference, we transmit the same attitude to others. As a Spanish proverb puts it, "If you live with wolves, you will learn to howl."[25]

148

Most of us realize the value and importance of example, but the challenge is to live as we know we should. How many times have we heard someone say, "Do as I say, not as I do." Yet, it is what we do, not what we say, that carries the greatest influence.

There are those who believe that what they do is of no concern of others. But life is not lived that way. What they do—what we all do—hurts or helps others whether we want it to or not.

If we are to be responsible individuals, if we are to live any measure of the Savior's admonition to love one another, and if we are truly concerned about our families, our communities, and our nation, then we must be willing to accept the responsibility of exemplary living.

We are now beginning a new year, a time often used to set our annual bench marks. We call them New Year resolutions. And one of the most meaningful resolutions has been suggested by the greatest Exemplar of all. The Lord said, "Let your light so shine before men, that they may see your good works, and glorify your Father which is in heaven."[24]

In the words of the hymn, "Come, let us anew; our journey pursue;...And our talents improve By the patience of hope and the labor of love..."[25] so that this year, and always, we may be a model for good, not only in what we say, but in all we do.   JANUARY 7, 1973

"Born Free to Follow Your Heart"

Like the lion cubs written of in the song "Born Free," man also has an inner need to "follow [his] heart." We call it conviction—the belief and testimony which gives us the courage to challenge life.

Conviction does not come easily. There will always be those who have a differing point of view, and to be able to decide for ourselves, to establish our own operating principles, is a part of being born free.

The varying options will always create divisions. At best, we will find others willing to share our convictions; at worst, we will stand alone, perhaps even find it necessary to defend our belief at the peril of our life. And it is when we stand alone that we examine our position most carefully. There is not much challenge in accepting what everyone else accepts; the difficulty comes in defending an unpopular viewpoint—especially defending it to ourselves.

And part of that challenge is to know one is right. No one wants to be wrong, but determining what is right requires soul-searching effort. Sometimes both sides are right, or partially right; sometimes neither side. And so each of us must arrive at our own conclusions, develop our own convictions. If we are sincere in our effort, we will not rely solely on logic, but will make prayer part of the process. To develop convictions without the guidance of the Holy Spirit is as senseless as sailing without a compass.

There is another important point to remember: we cannot condemn a man because he disagrees with us. He may be wrong, but we should give him credit for defending his beliefs. No one should be faulted for acting in a way he honestly believes he should. Leaders are often placed in the precarious position of carrying out the will of the people while not violating their own personal beliefs. Sometimes there is no choice, as one's conscience will not allow him to do other than what his convictions dictate.

Developing strong convictions is a character-building exercise. It means we must have the courage to stand up in defense of what we believe, to change when we find we are wrong, and to allow all men everywhere the same privilege. OCTOBER 28, 1973

14

SUCCESS REQUIRES PERSISTENCE AND PERSEVERANCE

success | dreams | accomplishments

*The talent of success
is nothing more than
doing what you can well,
and doing well
whatever you do,
without a thought of fame.*

HENRY WADSWORTH LONGFELLOW

Success Requires Persistence and Perseverance

The dreams and hopes we all have in life will never be realized by just waiting and hoping they'll come true. It takes an effort on our part. If we are to accomplish anything we must be willing to accept the challenge of searching, waiting, trying, perhaps failing, and trying again. Success requires a constant effort, a perseverance every day of our lives. Yet, too often we are willing to give up too easily—to leave the challenge for someone else.

Today's modern living tends to make spectators of us rather than doers. It is much easier to watch a ball game than to play in one, and it's easier yet to watch it on television than attend it in person. In each case the rewards are less.

And so it is with everything we do. It is easier to watch someone else bake a cake, or plant a garden, or climb a mountain than it is to do it or attempt it ourselves. But nothing in life can replace the thrill of accomplishment, or the satisfaction of knowing we met the challenge head-on and did our best.

When we do try, when we decide to do something, or set out to meet a challenge or opportunity, we need also to be aware that we may meet with early disappointment. And if we do, we need also to be aware that we can conquer it with persistence and perseverance.

That is not to say that there are not times when a challenge may be too big for us for one reason or another. Sydney Harris said, "...beating your head against a wall is more likely to produce a concussion in the head than a hole in the wall."[1] But the greater danger is to give up too soon.

When we leave a task unfinished it gnaws at us from the inside. An unfinished diet, an unfinished book or unfinished work leaves us with an unfinished feeling and sometimes a fear to try again.

We owe it to ourselves to try every day of our lives to make our dreams come true. But it requires persistence and perseverance. As Carlyle said, "Every noble work is at first impossible."[2]

The Opportunity for New Ideas

It is reassuring to know that no one has an exclusive corner on fresh and innovative ideas. The opportunity to generate new thought is open to us all.

What is unfortunate, however, is that there are so many who feel that there are restrictions—either on themselves, because they lack confidence in their ability to be creative, or an imposed restriction on others, who, they believe, are not qualified to originate new ideas. Both are wrong. New ideas can come from anyone at any time.

Creative thinking is like anything else worth achieving. It requires effort and hard work. But if we tell ourselves we are not capable of generating original ideas, we will soon begin to believe it. And if we make no effort we will see no results.

Some argue that there is no such thing as a new idea, that everything is a repeat of something that has gone before. As one suggests, "No man can establish title to an idea—at the most he can only claim possession."[3] Perhaps in some ways that is true because we do borrow from the experiences of others, as well as the events and people and places in our own lives. But the way in which we assimilate the events and experiences that comprise our individual life is genuinely original with us. No one else sees things exactly as we do because no one else has had our identical

154

experiences, our perspective. This has a snowball effect in productive thinking: We can pick up a good idea, add some of our own thoughts—our own being—and give birth to yet *another* new idea.

We must also be willing to accept the ideas of others, for a negative attitude toward someone can be a deterrent to new thought. The most progressive and innovative organizations are continually looking for input from all sources. A business executive recently confided that some of his best ideas came from office boys or messengers.

And so it is in our personal lives and in our homes. The closest and most successful family is the one that accepts ideas and input from all its members. We all need to be open to new ideas from those around us and believe in our ability to generate a few of our own.   APRIL 28, 1974

The Efficiency of Simplicity

Simplicity is a trait worth developing in ourselves and worth looking for in others. It brings about greater efficiency, which, according to a Canadian writer, gets things done in the smoothest possible way, with the least wear and tear, and the smallest expenditure of energy.[4]

Efficiency is often nothing more than finding a better way to do the same old task. And since that often means simplifying our procedure, simplicity is one of the tools of greater efficiency.

Simplicity can be achieved through selective concentration. Thomas Carlyle observed, "The weakest living creature, by concentrating his powers on a single object, can accomplish something; the strongest, by dispersing his [power] over many [objects], may fail to accomplish anything."[5]

No difficult problem is ever conquered by trying to tackle all aspects of it at once. First, the non-essential parts must be eliminated, and the problem approached one step at a time. We will find that we are more efficient when we keep an assignment simple, when we cut off waste and intensify concentration.

Indeed, simplicity is a worthy trait to develop for it applies to all aspects of life. William George Jordan has pointed out that even "Nature, in all her revelations, seeks to teach man the greatness of simplicity. Health is but the living of a physical life in harmony with a few simple, clearly defined laws. Simple food, simple exercise, simple precautions will work wonders," he said.[6]

In order to achieve efficient simplicity, we must be willing to reject or surrender habits and ways of life that are keeping us from higher things. Again said Jordan: "Reform your diet and you simplify it; make your speech truer and higher and you simplify it; reform your morals and you begin to cut off your immorals. The secret of all true greatness is simplicity."[6]

It would, therefore, be wise for us all to begin to cultivate simplicity in all things in order that our lives be more efficient.   APRIL 21, 1974

...For the Right Reasons

Nearly all our activities in life are triggered by one force or another, whether it's work or recreation, or even meeting such basic needs as eating and sleeping. All occur because of some inner or outer motivation which moves us to action. The challenge is to acquire control over these impulses so that we will do the *right* thing for the *right* reasons.

156

There are many people who regret their influence and positions in life because they sought them for the wrong reasons. Sometimes we are fooled into believing that our actions are for a worthy cause when, in fact, the true motivation was for a dishonest or unethical purpose. When that's the case, we will usually discover one of two basic drives behind it—power or money.

A national newspaper columnist once observed that the desire for power leads the list of motivating forces. "Men will do for power," he said, "what they will not do for money."[7] Still, money is the most popular motivating force. There are more people who go astray chasing the almighty dollar than there are who falter in search of power.

We recently spoke of the need for a strong work ethic and the value of doing honest work. A key point was that if we work solely for monetary reward without a sense of accomplishment, unhappiness will surely follow.

As members of this year's graduating class begin to make decisions concerning their future, we would suggest that their decisions be based on something more than financial rewards. There is more to happiness than a large bank account—more to life than what money can buy. Now we recognize the need and value of a properly motivated economic system and need for an adequate income. The homes we live in, the clothes we wear, the places we go and the way we get there—all involve a monetary exchange. But we must still be cautious and not allow money to become our prime inducement.

Fortunately, many do understand the need for additional goals in life: good works, personal achievements, pride, and love of fellowman. Without proper motivations, life would become meaningless.

157

There are many things in life which motivate us, but we must acquire control over our impulses lest we pursue our ambitions for the wrong reasons.   JUNE 9, 1974

"If Only I Were Rich..."

"If only I were rich..." Most of us are not strangers to that wishful thought, as we have no doubt contemplated what we could do with an unlimited bank account. Agreed, there are those who truly do need more, and those who try desperately to survive on what little they have. To these individuals most of us are regarded as prosperous—for our daydreams are usually centered on our wants rather than our needs.

The yardstick by which prosperity is often measured is somewhat analogous to what was once called covetousness — in the material wealth we want to acquire rather than what we already have.

Take food, for instance. Few of us can begin to image the grinding hunger which plagues millions daily, or the starvation which takes many lives each year. As Oliver Cromwell once wrote, "Some men have food, but no appetite; others have appetite, but no food; I have both. The Lord be thanked."[8] Truly, we who have enough to eat should also thank the Lord, for we are rich compared to many of our fellowmen.

It would also be well to recall the life-style of America's early settlers some two hundred years ago. Work was physical, hard and long—and usually dangerous. Childbearing was a major threat to the life of both mother and child. Epidemics destroyed entire populations. Medical science was rudimentary, and surgery often a greater threat to life than the illness. Yes, life was short and precarious.

Against this background, we begin to feel richer than we supposed, and it becomes obvious that the real riches in life are not to be found in bank balances.

Indeed, what is the meaning of the word "rich"? If we are honest with ourselves, we will realize that the only meaningful wealth we can acquire is something that cannot be purchased, or measured in dollars, or material possessions—inner peace. And inner peace can only come from within through the discovery, discipline and conquest of self. APRIL 27, 1975

The Triumph of Enthusiasm

Enthusiasm is one of life's great elixirs. As Charles Kingsley noted, "...all that we need to make us really happy is something to be enthusiastic about."[9] And there is nothing better to generate enthusiasm than life itself.

Often we see the spontaneous fervor of young children at play and watch the excitement permeate their entire being. And so it should be, for enthusiasm is a natural part of life. But like all values, it must be cared for or it will lose its regenerative powers.

When we are young, life is full of new experiences which help us grow. We are constantly reinforced with our successes; our enthusiasm is high. But as we grow older and experience failure and disappointment, our enthusiasm often withers. But this, too, is a part of life and we must be prepared to overcome it. If we do not nurture our enthusiasm, indifference will set in and life will lose much of its attraction.

Three thoughts come to mind as possible sources for retaining this valuable emotion. First, enthusiasm often depends on attitude. Some people are old at twenty while others are young at sixty, simply because of their approach to life.

Second, much of our enthusiasm in life can come from an understanding of who we are, and of our relationship with God. The ancient Greeks taught that God is in each of us, and that we are inspired by Him. Certainly, it is the gentle touch of the Lord that keeps many individuals in tune with the world, and brings joy and purpose to their lives.

Finally, we would suggest that enthusiasm can even come from an awareness of simple beauties in the world around us, and the courage to appreciate them even when the future is uncertain.

Indeed, as Van Dyke suggested, we must "...never lose life's zest, because the road's last turn will be the best."[10]

MARCH 2, 1975

Failure Is Never Final

Life would probably be much simpler if each of us knew what the future holds. It would allow us to avoid many of life's trouble spots through careful planning. But life was not intended to be trouble-free, and we must therefore, as the song says, "press on...though deepening trials throng [our] way."[11]

As we have said before, life does contain difficult moments, and deepening trials of various sorts are very much a part of our existence. We cannot escape them. We must conquer them or risk defeat. Yes, for some the hurdles are higher and more frequent, while others seem to run an almost effortless race. But obstacles exist for everyone, and if we quit when the going gets rough, our achievements will have little significance.

History proves that most major contributions were accomplished in the face of overwhelming odds or repeated defeats. There are thousands of examples, such as Abraham Lincoln's failure-plagued rise to the U.S. Presidency. Time and again he was defeated, yet in the face of defeat and failure, he eventually achieved success and undying fame to the end of time.

Life is like that. The capacity of our minds and bodies is much greater than we imagine, and unconsciously we draw upon this reservoir of mental and physical strength when we are faced with great difficulties.

Recently a mother on a river-running excursion with her family suddenly saw her four-year-old son thrown out of the boat and into the swirling, icy water. Desperately she lunged for the boy's foot as he disappeared beneath the water, but the current was too strong and he slipped from her grasp. A split second later the boy's foot appeared, and this time, with more speed and strength than she knew was possible, the mother fastened a determined hold that no river could tear loose. Soon the boy was back in the boat. Here was a woman who rallied courageously in the face of defeat—and won.

And so with all of us. No matter who we are, challenges of all sizes await us. Some we will handle with ease while others will push us to or even beyond our limit. But still the thing to remember is that we can conquer them if we will but press on with courage.   JUNE 23, 1974

"Who's Losing?"

One of life's reassuring truths is the knowledge that we are free to set our own course here upon the Earth. We must "lift [our] eyes to the [Lord from] whence cometh [our] help,"[12] but our Father in heaven expects us to shoulder much of the responsibility that comes with our free agency. It means we must be willing to try, to believe we can overcome difficulty; for a positive mental attitude is the thermostat that regulates what we accomplish in life.

If we are positive, objective and optimistic in our thinking, we will find new challenges and new victories as our constant companions. The story is told of a man who, when asked if he could play the piano, replied, "I don't know; I never tried."[13]

Attitude is what counts most. Church leader Marvin Ashton recalls watching a professional baseball game when a fan who was late in arriving asked, "Who's losing?"

"Neither one," was the response. The man glanced at the scoreboard and saw the game was not tied. He walked on, but was undoubtedly curious about the answer he received.

"Some of us are ahead," said Mr. Ashton, "and some are behind, but no one is losing. All of us...will do well to realize that attitude is more important than the score."[14]

We can overcome fear with a positive attitude. We can accomplish the difficult, find answers to the impossible, and defeat the undefeatable. There is nothing magical nor mystical about the power of belief. The how-to-do-it always comes to the person who believes he can do it.

John Heron wrote, "All the progress of civilization is due to the constructive thinking of people. The record of history is brilliant with the deeds of men and women who said 'I can,' while it is silent for the most part concerning those who said 'I can't.' Positive people believe that it is better to fail in carrying out a project than to not fail because they have not tried."[13]

Knowing our goals and objectives and making a commitment to reach them is the only way life will have meaning for us. A sincere desire to achieve something requires more than a simple willingness to receive it. Achievement comes from purposeful, energetic, and creative perseverance, with an eye single to the goal.

Great works and great moments are often performed not by strength but by positive perseverance. Indeed, as one spiritual leader said, "We make our own choice, we sow our own seed, we harvest our own crop...it is ours to decide."[15]

JANUARY 5, 1975

"...Keep on Being a Success'

"One thing is forever good"; said Emerson, and "That one thing is Success."[16] There is a great exhilaration which comes to one through honest, well-earned achievement. To plan well, work hard and persist to the end brings one of life's sweetest rewards: the feeling of accomplishment.

We all desire and hope to succeed—and everyone does, though sometimes we fail to recognize it. Too often success is thought of in terms of money, prestige and authority; yet success can come in all things and to anyone doing any task. As Longfellow said, "The talent of success is nothing more than doing what you can well; and doing well whatever you do, without a thought of fame."[17]

Success seldom comes easy. Whatever our goal, it is bound to be wrought with frustration and hardship. If a task were easy, success would have little meaning. Indeed, the greater the degree of success we enjoy, the greater the degree of difficulty needed to accomplish the work. And not only does it require much work, but much preparation as well. Again, quoting Emerson, "...success depends upon previous preparation, and without such preparation there is sure to be failure."[18]

Failure itself is not always bad, for therein we learn, progress, and gain appreciation for success. What is bad is failure which turns to defeat and discourages us from trying again; or success which turns to conceit and leaves us with the impression that we have no further need to succeed.

One of the dangers in achieving success comes in the failure to realize that it is fleeting—for the moment only—and gradually fades away, needing to be replaced with new successes. When we set a goal there is hope, excitement and challenge. When we reach that goal there is pride of accomplishment and the necessity to set new sights. Henry Ward Beecher said, "Success is full of promise till men get it; and then it is a last-year's nest from which the birds have flown."[19]

We all need success in life and we need it continually. That is the challenge, for as Irving Berlin said, "The toughest part about being a success is that you've got to keep on being a success."[20]   NOVEMBER 12, 1972

Milestones Are Not Finish Lines

As each of us pass through this time-measured existence on earth, our lives are marked with significant times and events: birthdays, anniversaries, graduations, promotions all are milestones that serve as reference points. They pinpoint our successes and failures, mark our beginnings and turning points, and provide targets and guildelines for new goals.

With this broadcast, the Mormon Tabernacle Choir observes an important milestone in its own history. Today the Choir completes forty-five years of nationwide singing to countless millions via the broadcast media. Thousands of people have been involved in these broadcasts—each contributing in various ways to the messages and feelings which have been shared through music. And it has not been without effort, for, as Josiah G. Holland wrote: "There is no royal road to anything—One thing at a time, and all things in succession. That which grows slowly endures."[21]

And so as we stand at this marker and reflect on these past forty-five years, we are reminded of the enduring success that has come from the efforts of many. We are also reminded that milestones are not finish lines. Too often we think of key events as the beginning, or the end, when in reality they only represent a continuation.

The runner in a race does not stop at the three-quarter-mile post, but uses that marker to measure his pace and effort. So it should be with each of us as we pass our own landmarks. Rather than viewing them as finish lines, we should regard them as the beginning of new challenges and horizons. And if the challenge seems beyond our grasp, we should remember the words of Robert Browning: "...a man's reach should exceed his grasp,..."[22]

Yes, milestones tell us where we've been, where we are and where we are going. Life's greatest moments are only markers along an eternal road.   JULY 14, 1974

15

WORRY— THE GREAT AMERICAN DISEASE

worry | problems | disappointment | optimism

courage and victory

*Life is a constant
problem-solving affair,
but each of us has deep within us
the blessing of opportunity—
no matter how heavy our burdens or
how perplexing our difficulties—
to think through and solve our problems.*

Worry—the Great
American Disease

Trouble and difficulty are a real and necessary part of our existence, for without them there are many lessons in life we would fail to learn. As poet Robert Hamilton said:

> *I walked a mile with Sorrow*
> *And ne'er a word said she;*
> *But, oh, the things I learned from her*
> *When Sorrow walked with me.*[1]

But with our sorrow comes also worry—worry of what to do about our difficulties and how to overcome them.

Worry has been described as the great American disease. It causes much unhappiness and is one of the least productive activities we have. Worry can impair our appetite, disturb our sleep, and irritate our disposition. As we have said before, there is a vast difference between thinking about our problems and worrying about them.

But an even more wasteful activity is worrying about problems that are nonexistent. Mark Twain said, "I am an old man and have known a great many troubles, but most of them have never happened."[2] To worry about events that may never occur is to lose faith in life. In his meditations, Marcus Aurelius wrote: "Nothing happens to anybody which he is not fitted by nature to bear."[3]

Someone has mathematically calculated that forty percent of our worries will never materialize, thirty percent deal with old decisions which cannot be changed, twelve percent focus on criticism which is mostly untrue, ten percent deal with our health which only worsens when we worry, and only eight percent is legitimate. The point we would make is that life does have real problems which may be met head-on when we eliminate useless and senseless worry.

167

It is God's plan for us to learn and progress, and troubles are part of our earthly schooling. Worry is life's truancy. The anticipation of trouble is often the cause of our real difficulties; or, as Seneca wrote, "He suffers more than is necessary, who suffers before it is necessary."[4]

Yes, troubles are a part of life, but worry is mental poison which paralyzes thought and action. We will have greater happiness if we will use a simple, common-sense approach to the business of life and leave our worries by the wayside.   SEPTEMBER 29, 1974

Expect the Unexpected

It has been said that "Obstacles bring out the best in resourceful people."[5]   And although we do not seek difficulty or disappointment, we all must face them to some degree and at some time. A great comfort in such moments is the knowledge that we can, as the song suggests, "Lean on [His] ample arm."[6]

Yes, faith and prayer are important in overcoming difficulties. As we have said before, they are basic to the development of our character. But it is the ability to be resourceful which is necessary to overcome obstacles and find, in part, the answer to our prayers. It is through resourcefulness that we blaze new trails, discover new answers to old problems and overcome seemingly insurmountable barriers.

A resourceful person is one who has the ability to meet and handle a situation. We all like to believe we have that ability, but often we fall short because we fail to realize that to be resourceful means to be pliable—to be ready to adjust and make the best, and most, of any situation. Few things in life remain the same. Change is what our world is all about, and if we are going to be resourceful we must be willing to alter our plans to meet new circumstances and accommodate new needs. It is reported that when the automobile came into being, most of those who built buggies were absorbed into the new industry, but those who were unwilling to adjust soon found themselves out of work.

In addition, a resourceful person does not fear the unexpected. He knows that he cannot plan for every contingency, that he must keep flexible and have at his command the resourcefulness to adapt as the situation dictates.

Many "impossible dreams" have been accomplished by resourcefulness. In fact, there is an Armed Forces motto which says, "The difficult we do immediately; the impossible takes a little longer." And so, though we would hope that "hard times [would] come again no more"[7] they are a part of life. And if we make resourcefulness a part of our moral fiber, we will also be able to make the best of life's obstacles.   MARCH 4, 1973

Life Is a Problem-Solving Affair

Life for all of us has its problems. It has been said that life is a problem-solving existence which will defeat us if we let it. But is has also been said that no man ever sank under the burden of one day. It is when tomorrow's burden is added that the weight becomes unbearable.

We must take life a day at a time, and obstacles are a part of life. They help us learn and develop and improve in all we do.

Even as children, we soon discover that problems must be solved if we are to achieve our desires. As we grow older and become more involved with life, the problems

169

and obstacles increase. The boy who wants to go fishing with his father and has just been invited to play in the all-star game on the same day, has to cope with a problem. Or the young lady who has already promised to baby-sit for the neighbors, only to receive a long-awaited invitation for a special date, has a problem. And so it is—for each of us—every day. But if we face each problem and each day head-on, our ability to cope with adversity increases and new dimensions are added to our character. The final result is that life becomes more meaningful.

It is also well to remember that we learn and grow by solving problems, not by worrying about them. We often create many of our own complications by failing to keep life simple. We must brush worries and failures aside, or we may never get around to any solutions. Worry is a mental poison. It paralyzes thought and action.

Harold Walker said, "You can think about your problems or you can worry about them, and there is a vast difference between the two....Thinking works its way through problems to conclusions....When you worry, you go over the same ground endlessly and come out the same place you started. Thinking makes progress from one place to another; worry remains static. The problem of life is to change worry into thinking."[8]

Life is a constant problem-solving affair, but each of us has deep within us the blessing of opportunity—no matter how heavy our burdens or how perplexing our difficulties—to think through and solve our problems.

AUGUST 20, 1972

"When You Are Discouraged..."

Moments of discouragement come to everyone. They are a part of life. And although not always desired, they are

170

certainly to be expected. Harry Emerson Fosdick said, "One who expects completely to escape low moods is asking the impossible."[9] And so our challenge is not to live a life free of discouragement, but to know we can overcome it.

If there is an antidote for *dis*couragement, it may be the word's antonym, *en*couragement—both from others and from ourselves. One way *self*-encouragement can come is by recalling other difficulties we faced, remembering that we overcame them through faith and hard work—a step at a time.

Perhaps our greatest source of encouragement in fighting adversity comes from our Lord and Savior. Not only can we turn to Him for comfort and guidance, but we can also gain strength by remembering what He has already done for us. As J. Oatman said in verse: "When you are discouraged, thinking all is lost,...Count your many blessings; name them one by one,/And it will surprise you what the Lord has done..."[10] If counting our blessings helps us overcome discouragement it is because by doing so we realize we have had success and therein we find self-encouragement.

We should also remember those around us and their need for encouragement from us. We are seldom aware of the problems or pressures others face. Longfellow said, "Every man has his secret sorrow which the world knows not; and often-times we call a man cold when he is only sad."[11] Someone else's need for encouragement from us might be greater than we will ever know. Appreciative understanding and a sincere word of praise to others can be a great source of strength and comfort.

But the greatest comfort of all is to know that the Savior is willing and waiting to help. No matter how big our problem or how deep our despair, we can overcome discouragement if we will "cast [our] burden upon the Lord."[12]   OCTOBER 29, 1972

171

Champions of Courage

The brotherhood we share with each other is an important part of our lives for often it is from each other we gain the courage to carry on. So it is with two of this country's great presidents.

Both were men of unmatched courage and integrity. But in praising their accomplishments, we often forget to consider the setbacks they suffered, and the defeats which helped mold their characters. Washington experienced many reverses during the Revolutionary War before he rallied his weary troops to victory.

And Lincoln's biographers give us a long list of his early failures. His first candidacy for the legislature was unsuccessful. He entered the business world and failed, spending fifteen years of his life paying off the debts of a worthless partner. He ran for Congress and was badly defeated. He tried for an appointment to the U.S. Land Office and failed. He became a candidate for the vice-presidency and was again defeated.

Certainly, Lincoln must have been discouraged many times, but from each defeat he gained strength; from each failure he drew determination. Instead of allowing his defeats to push him down, he used them to pull himself up.

We all know the greatness of Washington and Lincoln. But we should learn more than greatness from these two men. We should learn humility and courage in the face of setbacks.

David O. McKay once said that adversity may provide a means of spiritual uplift. "Adversity itself," he said, "may lead toward and not away from God and spiritual enlightenment."[13]

Yes, if we were to examine the personal lives of successful people, we would find that most of them have also experienced failure, and have profited spiritually from it. It was another president, Theodore Roosevelt, who said: "Far better it is to dare mighty things, to win glorious triumphs, even though checkered by failure, than to take rank with those poor spirits who neither enjoy much nor suffer much, because they live in the gray twilight that knows not victory nor defeat."[14]

Epictetus put it more succinctly: "Difficulties are what show men's character."[15]

Washington and Lincoln showed their character not only by their great accomplishments but by their refusal to be intimidated by failure. We can admire them for their greatness, but we must try to emulate them for their courage in the face of defeat. For surely, "The greatest test of courage on the earth is to bear defeat without losing heart."[16]   FEBRUARY 9, 1975

We All Face Disappointments

One of the important lessons we learn in life is that we don't always get what we want when we want it—that disappointment is a normal experience in our learning process.

Life is filled with disappointments. Much of our time is spent solving the problems they present. Even the best plans and guarantees sometimes go awry.

In 1972, three men again journeyed to outer space, a task which required great preparation and detailed planning. But even as those men approached the very moment their flight was to begin, difficulties arose; and months, even years, of planning came to a halt. There was disappointment not only to the astronauts, but to the thousands who worked on the project and the millions more who watched or listened to the drama unfold. In this instance, the disappointment was short-lived and Apollo 17 was soon on its way headed for new challenges.

173

Similarly, there are times when we all face disappointments—both great and small. Whenever we take a trip and miss an appointment because of a travel delay, there is a letdown—a minor one to be sure, but one that must be faced, nevertheless, and adjustments made. So, too, we must face the major disillusionments of life, for if we do not learn to cope with small difficulties, the large ones will overwhelm us. Afterward, we must learn to forget them and remember only the wisdom they may provide.

None of us seek or want difficulties in life, but they can be useful tools for personal growth and the development of firm, integrated character. They can even become new opportunities. In fact, many times, these temporary setbacks have helped men find God and new reasons for living.

It is dangerous and unrealistic to believe that we can avoid disappointments in life—especially so for children. We should help them learn and understand that lesson before they become set in a mold of unreasonable expectation.

And so, as we review our blessings, it would be well for us to acknowledge disappointment as a potentially meaningful part of life on earth. When we accept that principle and properly apply it, disappointments can also be a blessing. DECEMBER 10, 1972

Fear of the Unknown

Fear of the unknown is a natural and common experience. We have all experienced anxieties that come from facing the inevitable events of the future: starting a new school year, venturing into a new business, moving to a new town, meeting a new person—all are experiences laced with a certain degree of apprehension.

But facing up to such challenges is the lifeblood of human growth and progress. It is always easier to live in

174

the past where we are comfortable with our mastery of the familiar, but our potential, our abilities, and the promise of a more satisfying tomorrow can best be nurtured with the challenge of an unnamed, unmet, unconquered future.

A former U.S. President once said, "The only limit to our realization of tomorrow will be our doubts of to-day."[17] History is replete with men and women who dared to meet their doubts and fears head-on; who overcame them, and thereby enriched their own lives, and in so doing, contributed to the betterment of all mankind.

Columbus ignored the doubts of his peers who declared the Earth flat, and sailed on to prove it was round. Our pioneer ancestors bravely faced untamed frontiers to lay the foundations for today's modern cities. And Jonas Salk believed polio could be prevented, but had to struggle past many defeats before it became a reality. As one writer observed, "Once men are caught up in an event they cease to be afraid."[18]

And so, as we face the inevitable yet unknown future, let us not sit back timidly, but push forward and allow ourselves to be caught up in the challenge of our work. It will be through our own efforts that we will defeat our doubts and fears and nourish the potential that is within us all. "It generally happens," wrote Samuel Johnson, "that assurance keeps an even pace with ability."[19] With each new experience we have, and with each new skill or understanding we gain, we also achieve self-confidence and added courage to meet the unknown future.

Indeed, "The only limit to our realization of to-morrow will be our doubts of today."[17]   SEPTEMBER 8, 1974

There Is No Cause for Panic

There are times in life when we are not sure what our next move should be, or what we should do in a certain situa-

175

tion. It is on these occasions—when the seriousness of the difficulty and the need for a quick response makes us uneasy—that many of us turn and run. But as Gandhi said, "Panic is the most demoralizing state anyone can be in."[20]

Through the ages men have panicked for many reasons, and the results have usually been negative. Panic is a sudden, overpowering fear, and fear makes us irrational and irresponsible. It is impossible to think clearly when we are in a state of panic.

To avoid the onset of this overpowering emotion, we must recognize some of the symptoms: a feeling of despair, the belief that there is no solution for our problems, the conviction that we are alone without help. Panic can occur suddenly, or it can build slowly and gradually erode our common sense, leaving us stranded with our imaginations running rampant.

Many recall the panic created by Orson Welles' *War of the Worlds*—a superb piece of fiction, but to many the fear it created was as real as if an invasion of Earth had actually occurred. When we don't have all the facts and we lose contact with the real world, panic sweeps in to take control.

True, a problem may exist, but it is often less serious than we imagine. Marie Curie said, "Nothing in life is to be feared. It is only to be understood."[21]

As we examine the world around us, it is easy for us to become frightened and panic. We observe the growing pollution, we read about the energy crisis, and experience fuel and food shortages. These are real problems, yes, but they are not solved with quick emotional responses. Solutions will be found and life will go on. As Epictetus said, we must make the best use of what is in our power, "and take the rest as it happens."[22] But to panic and take refuge from life is to refuse life itself.

It is often said that moderation in all things is good, and that certainly holds true for our emotions. To again quote the late Gandhi, "There never is any cause for panic. One must keep heart whatever happens."[20]   JULY 8, 1973

Modern Pioneers

In each of our lives there are moments when the windows of our world are covered with rain and gloom, when the spirit of challenge fades and we lose all motivation. It is not a new experience. Since the beginning of time men have been plagued with these feelings. They are unique to no one and often forcefully persist during climbs to new heights or the blazing of new trails.

Many times throughout history pioneers have found defeat and discouragement a more common partner than victory and optimism. That is a part of pioneering, and pioneering is a part of our lives.

Usually we visualize pioneers as traditional Western trail-blazers with covered wagons and prairie homes. To them the great challenge was simply survival, and for many it was a challenge that could not be met. We have had pioneers in every age, every nation, and every endeavor, and for each the challenge was no less.

The current mood seems to be that the age of pioneering is past. We have progressed so far in the past twenty years that some believe there is nothing left to invent, no new challenges to meet, no unexplored horizons to conquer. But the opposite is true. Men on the moon are not unlike those pioneers who traveled in covered wagons to conquer new frontiers. And certainly those who have found ways to cure or prevent deadly diseases rightfully belong to the class of modern pioneers.

177

But so do each of us. Every man in his own sphere faces the difficulty of passing through unexplored territory. No one has lived your life before. No one will have exactly the same choices to make. And so, in a sense, we are all pioneers faced with the challenge of controlling and conquering our own complex world. That is our pioneering heritage; that is our pioneering challenge, and hopefully when it is met we, too, will be able to say, "All is well! All is well!"

JULY 21, 1974

Afraid of the Dark

Wise and loving parents have often taught us not to fear the dark. Simply because our eyes do not perceive the familiar surroundings seen in daylight is no reason to fear our path is taking an unexpected turn into uncertainty. And so it is with life.

Too many view the future with apprehension, with a fear of facing the unknown, perhaps of something even ominous awaiting them. Many even suggest the best of life is past, that they never again will experience the good times they once knew. But gratefully such has not been life's pattern. Reality is seldom as bad as our imaginative fears.

Problems and uncertainty are not unique to our time. Our ancestors had no energy crisis, but then, neither did they have automobiles. Heating their homes and obtaining sufficient food supplies were usually tasks requiring considerable work and worry. Yet, they lived through their difficulties and discouragements—and we can live through ours.

Life will go on and take us with it, but like our darkened room, we will not, nor cannot, always perceive the future. We can, however, safely assume that familiar objects and landmarks are still there to guide us, not the least of which is a loving Heavenly Father.

As a nation, as families, as individuals, we need the wisdom, the courage, and honesty to face the facts, to profit from our mistakes, and not to let imagined fears or uncertainty dissipate and dispel our ability to tackle the future. Surely a people who have left footprints on the moon can find the answers to perplexing problems on this sphere, at this point in history.

Call it a new resolution, or a time to take stock. Call it repentance or simply not being afraid of the dark. Call it what you will, it still adds up to our need to be grateful for the privilege of life. Given the right frame of mind, we can profit from the experience of others and from our own mistakes. And with the Lord's help, we can give meaning and purpose to the future. For a future there will always be, and we can meet it knowing it has been met and conquered by others before us.

JANUARY 12, 1975

179

16

SWEET IS THE WORK

work | success | sacrifice

service | goals | rewards

*There is a...nobleness and
even sacredness, in Work....
Even in the meanest sorts of Labour,
the whole soul of man is
composed into a kind of real harmony
the instant he sets himself to work.*

THOMAS CARLYLE

180

"Sweet Is the Work"

Most of us have foolishly thought, at one time or another, that life would be ideal if we didn't have to work. But it is not so. Work is the measure of success in everyday life, it is a remedy for sickness of the soul; and to know how to perform honest work is one of the most valuable lessons we can learn.

Yes, work is a necessary part of our existence. Some of the moments we remember best are of hours when we worked the hardest. But to spend all of our time working without stopping to relax is just as harmful as spending all of our time in recreational pursuits. We all enjoy a well-earned relief from work—the pleasant, self-satisfying relaxation which comes after giving our all in hard work. Both labor and leisure are needful for physical and emotional balance—each makes the other more valuable and worthwhile. But too often we work begrudgingly, seeking only recreation. And sadly, far too many spend their entire lives this way. How much more rewarding it would be to accept work as an important and necessary part of life.

"There is a...nobleness," said Carlyle, "and even sacredness, in Work.... Even in the meanest sorts of Labour, the whole soul of man is composed into a kind of real harmony the instant he sets himself to work."[1]

Yes, steady, quiet, persistent work cannot be imitated or replaced. And of all the work we do, none should be more enjoyable or rewarding than the work we do for the Lord. A church leader recently stated that "...to serve God is the greatest career in the world."[2] We should also remember that when we spend part of our life furthering His kingdom on earth, it is a work that carries its own restorative powers.

The Lord said, "Come unto me, all ye that labour and are heavy laden, and I will give you rest. Take my yoke upon you, and learn of me;...For my yoke is easy, and my burden is light."[3]

Work can be rewarding, and especially—in the words of the hymn—"Sweet is the work, my God, my King, To praise thy name..."[4]

OCTOBER 14, 1973

"Man Is a Worker"

There are many who argue that the value of work and the work ethic are standards of the past that no longer apply in today's world. Some point to isolated cases of employee dissatisfaction or high turnover rates and absenteeism as proof that the majority are dedicated to avoiding work. While that may be true in some cases, it would seem that most people still rightfully recognize the value of honest work. Indeed, work is one of life's greatest blessings.

Charles Kingsley said that we should "thank God every morning when [we] get up that [we] have something to do that day which must be done, whether [we] like it or not."[5]

We all have our work. It is a key component to a satisfying life. When St. James said "...faith without works is dead,"[6] he might well have added that life without work is also meaningless.

In modern society there is a vast variety of work to be done, and we must be careful not to foolishly exalt one man's work above another's. All work is important or there would be no demand for it. Also, we must remember that the value of work encompasses much more than just the time or effort for which we are monetarily compensated. Volunteer work often augments the regular work we do for a living, and in the process increases the satisfaction we achieve in life through work.

Surely, we would all be happier if we could look for more satisfaction and meaning in our work instead of for its financial rewards only. Work sometimes is difficult and tedious, and if our only motivation is money, then it can also be detested.

Even the work of genius is sometimes tedious. Jane Ellice Hopkins said, "Genius is the capacity for taking infinite pains."[7] And Michelangelo added his own point of view when he remarked, "If people knew how hard I have to work to gain my mastery, it would not seem wonderful at all."[8] Usually, we need to look at the results of our work and not just the process if we want to understand its importance.

Yes, work is here to stay, and for that we are grateful; for work is truly one of life's great blessings. It has been said that "the world is governed and kept going by a few strong instincts; but among these not the least is that feeling that cannot be sponged from the human heart, the feeling that [we] have work to do..."[9]

As Joseph Conrad wrote: "A man is a worker. If he is not that he is nothing."[10] JUNE 2, 1974

"Where the Willingness Is Great..."

There is great comfort offered to mankind in the 23rd Psalm—the comfort in knowing that our Maker is willing to guide and direct us through troubled times. But we must always remember that His willingness to help us is directly related to our willingness to keep His commandments. And so it is with much that we do in life. The things we accomplish are directly related to our willingness to sacrifice and labor for them.

183

When the vast frontiers of America were settled there were many who wanted a part of the new land, but who were unwilling to make the sacrifice, to put forth the necessary effort.

We often set goals for ourselves and our families, but then back away when we are faced with the obstacles that must be overcome. We must remember that our attitude—our willingness—will help us overcome many of these hurdles.

Nearly five centuries ago Machiavelli wrote, "Where the willingness is great, the difficulties cannot be great."[11] And closer to our own time, Theodore Roosevelt added, "it is only through labor and painful effort, by grim energy and resolute courage, that we move on to better things." [12]

Often, willingness alone is all that is needed to set a great movement in motion. Many of the accomplishments of our pioneer forefathers came about through sheer desire and the realization that someone must take the lead. It was that kind of determination which made it possible for them to overcome seemingly insurmountable obstacles.

If we are to achieve, we must be willing to pay the price. We must be willing to take the initiative; willing to learn, to obey, to persevere; even willing to fail. Willingness—that is the key to all our accomplishments. Without it, we may never begin. With it, we may achieve more than we ever thought possible. It is a lesson that must be learned, hopefully, early in life. As John Heywood observed, "Nothing is impossible to a willing heart."[13]

JULY 16, 1972

"...No Toil Nor Labor Fear"

One-hundred-twenty-five years ago, Mormon pioneers began arriving in the Great Salt Lake Valley. They knew the necessity of hard work if they were to succeed in their new desert home; indeed, if they were even to survive. It was a reality pioneers of every age have known.

The Utah settlers were bolstered by a song written by one of their number. The words not only promised happiness, but reminded them not to be discouraged by hard work. "...no toil nor labor fear"[14] was the advice given—words which would be well for us all to remember.

The man who led the group westward, Brigham Young, told his fellow-pioneers, "Each will find that happiness in this world mainly depends on the work he does, and the way in which he does it."[15]

The opportunity and ability to work is a blessing that makes life worthwhile. The hours we usually remember best, the hours we are proudest of and cherish most are those in which we worked hardest. Even our recreation and vacation time is more enjoyable when work precedes it. A permanent vacation would soon loose its appeal and become a meaningless existence. In other words, recreation is a counterpart of work; neither is of much value without the other. Labor puts meaning into our achievements.

Unfortunately, we often waste valuable time and effort avoiding work. We expend more energy in trying to escape it than if we had completed the task in the first place. Procrastination is often no more than a fear of work. Wrote one unknown author, "Hard work never killed a man, but it sure has scared a lot of them."[16]

The hymn, "Come, Come, Ye Saints," was a lyrical plea for the pioneers to work hard at difficult tasks, and to enjoy the satisfaction that comes therein. That same challenge exists today for all of us, and if we respond successfully, we, too, will be able to say "All is well!"

Come, come, ye Saints, no toil nor labor fear,
But with joy wend your way;

Tho' hard to you this journey may appear,
Grace shall be as your day.
'Tis better far for us to strive
Our useless cares from us to drive;
Do this, and joy your hearts will swell—
All is well! All is well!...

JULY 23, 1972

"Lady Luck"

Each of us experience events in our lives which we could attribute to good or bad fortune. If we let ourselves—and there are many who do—we could believe that the results of nearly everything we do are based on chance. But usually, luck has little or nothing to do with our experiences in life.

Often we call a person lucky if he succeeds in business, just as the fisherman who catches his limit is thought to have luck on his side. But for those not so successful we believe them to be unlucky. In both cases, as with most of what we do, ability, skill and the application of correct principles usually have more to do with success or failure than does "Lady Luck." "Shallow men believe in luck," wrote Emerson, "...strong men believe in cause and effect."[16]

We carry the notions of good and bad luck with us from childhood: find a four-leaf clover, don't step on the cracks in the walk, hang a horseshoe over the door, don't walk under a ladder. These are all ideas which follow us into adulthood with a lingering influence. How many have said, "I don't believe in a rabbit's foot bringing good luck, but I'll carry one just in case?"

Certainly many things occur which appear to be attributable only to good or bad fortune. Because we do not understand why an event occurs does not mean there is no reason. We are deceived and in danger when we begin relying on luck, and develop a philosophy of chance. Most of what happens in life happens for a reason, though we may not know what it is. As one prophet wrote, "There is a law, irrevocably decreed in heaven...upon which all blessings are predicated—And when we obtain any blessing from God, it is by obedience to that law upon which it is predicated."[17]

The rewards of eternal life will not be determined by luck, nor will our happiness in this world. Both must be earned from within.   SEPTEMBER 9, 1973

A Change of Pace

One of life's certainties is that at some time or other each of us will get tired of what we are doing. Restlessness and fatigue are a natural part of life. As one doctor stated, "There is no way in which an ambitious and conscientious person can escape being tired and worn out—he just has to learn to accept it."[18]

Just as we must learn to understand and accept occasional fatigue, we must also realize that we have been given the mechanisms to combat it. One of the most fundamental methods of restoring efficiency is to do something different—to give ourselves a change of pace.

The old adage that a change is as good as a rest has merit. None of us can work steadily at the same task with consistent effectiveness. Even those individuals in occupations which require constant repetition require frequent breaks or changes in routine. And for years educational psychologists have told us that our capacity to learn decreases as the hours we sit and study grow longer. Our concentrated efforts soon reach a point of diminishing returns.

So it is in life. Without an occasional break in our routine we become stale and ineffective.

Columnist Sydney Harris once observed that "Relaxation, in its best sense, is not four hours put aside every [weekend] for golf. It is not a solid chunk of time hacked out of a busy week, in which one relaxes as furiously and intensely as one conducts business affairs.

"When work presses down most heavily," he continued, "a ten-minute walk, or a quiet moment with a crossword puzzle can restore efficiency to an amazing degree."[19] At home the remedy for fatigue might be light reading, working on a favorite hobby, or simply tackling a different project.

A popular saying is, "If you want to get something done, give it to a busy man." The truth in that statement lies partially in the fact that new challenges to a busy person often serve as a temporary release from regular assignments.

We all experience a bad day now and again, but if we seem to be having more than our share, perhaps the best remedy is to give ourselves a simple change of pace.

DECEMBER 2, 1973

Profiting From Good Advice

We would all do well to "listen to a prophet's voice, And hear the word of God"[20] for there is none among us so sure of his position in life that he could not profit from inspired guidance.

Daily we are bombarded with advice in every conceivable form and from every possible direction. There is never a shortage of advice, but there *is* constant need for honest and helpful suggestions. Part of our challenge, therefore, is to be discriminating in the counsel we select and heed so that we will implement only the most beneficial and helpful ideas.

188

Sophocles once warned that "No enemy is worse than bad advice."[21] Wherever we go we will find those who are willing to give unwise counsel. Sometimes it is in their own self-interest. Other times they mean well, but are not aware of the harm their advice may bring. It is up to each of us to weigh and carefully consider what is given. As John Collins said, "To profit from good advice requires more wisdom than to give it."[22]

Occasionally we feel there is safety in numbers and we are tempted to believe that if many people are saying the same thing then perhaps they are right. Perhaps they are. But we must be cautious, for it is also possible they may be wrong. To paraphrase a well-worn adage, if ten thousand people give bad advice, it is still bad advice. We must always carefully consider the source of counsel, for that is, perhaps, as important as the counsel itself.

Indeed, we need a bright, steady beacon to guide our course. But we must be sure that the light we are following comes from a beacon and not another ship off course, or a house along a rocky shore.

Perhaps all of us have, on occasion, become lost or confused in unfamiliar surroundings only to have the condition worsened by approaching darkness. Life is often that way, and it is at such times that we seek help most fervently. It is then that we are also most vulnerable to misdirection. But we would repeat from the Master's counsel, that no man is left alone to make his decisions. "Ask, and it shall be given you"; He said, "seek, and ye shall find; knock, and it shall be opened unto you."[23] As Gandhi has reminded us, "Divine guidance often comes when the horizon is the blackest."[24]

Yes, advice is a plentiful commodity in life; yet, good advice is a rare and precious light that will guide us through life's stormy channels.   OCTOBER 20, 1974

The Lay-Away Plan

Despite obvious appeal, most of us eventually learn that we cannot get something for nothing. But still we hear, and often give in to, the tempting invitation to "buy now—pay later." It's the second half—the pay-later part—that will return to haunt us if we do not fully understand its implications. Despite the enticing words, "consolidate your debts," we soon discover that "consolidate" does not mean obliterate. And when we act upon the assurance of "no payments due until the middle of next month," we find that the middle of next month does come and usually sooner than we expected.

Yes, the ability or willingness to postpone our desires is evidence of maturity. Impulse-buying often leads us to spend more than we earn, which is one reason why stores often assume a parental role by providing lay-away plans. The much desired merchandise is placed on a "high shelf" and kept out of our reach until it is fully paid for.

Not only is the something for nothing concept misleading in the commercial world, but it is a powerful and appealing illusion in all that we do. No child has ever walked the first time he took a step; no athlete has run the four-minute mile without first building endurance; no musician has ever performed at Carnegie Hall without years of study and practice. In fact, all the significant rewards of life are offered to us on the "lay-away" rather than the "enjoy-now, pay-later" plan.

Certainly there are options without immediate price tags which seemingly offer easier and less restrictive choices: submitting to peer pressure, quitting school, wasting time, using drugs or alcohol. But unfortunately, these "counterfeit bargains" usually exact a higher price in the long run. Although they promise much at the moment, they are paid for later with disappointment, sorrow and despair—perhaps even tragedy.

God and Heaven also are not obtained on the something-for-nothing plan. The Lord has clearly stated that faith and works are the prerequisites for spiritual rewards, that the promise of Heaven comes only to those who first do the will of Heaven.

Deciding what we want in life requires that we place our righteous goals in "lay-away"—on a high shelf but in clear view—and then work to pay the price before we seek to enjoy the product. The sooner we develop this kind of maturity and realize there is no such thing as "something for nothing," the sooner we will find joy and spiritual prosperity.   MARCH 23, 1975

17

"LOOK TO THIS DAY"

time | hope | change

youth | age | memories

*Today is yet another day,
a new opportunity to decide
how we will apply our gift of freedom.
It may be wasted, or
it may be used to accomplish
some lasting good.*

192

"Look to This Day"

"To everything there is a season,...A time to be born...a time to die;..."[1] And, may we add, a time to live, and that time is NOW! "Look to this day," is written in Sanskrit, "for it is life, the very life of life." Too often we are not content with the moment and wish it to rush on. Too often we wish the present hour would pass so we could hurry to the next, and hope that it, too, will quickly pass.

Youth is a time for storing up great treasures of life, yet the young are always in a hurry to be older. That is not to say the future is not important and that we should not prepare for it, but today is the time to think about tomorrow. Age is a time for benefitting from much experience, yet too many of the elderly long for their youth and simply wait for time to pass.

It does little good to hurry through life, if that's all we're doing. We spend so much of life wishing it away. At fourteen, we wish we were sixteen in order to drive; at sixteen, eighteen is our goal, so as to be out of high school; comes eighteen and college, and a desire to be married and have a family. When that day comes, it's "Oh, if the children were grown, we'd have more time to do what we want." After they are gone, and another wish that they were back, it's hurry on to retirement. And finally, we reach retirement and suddenly realize we have been so busy hurrying through life, we've failed to plan for that day and don't know what to do with it.

Cicero said: "For just as I approve of a young man in whom there is a touch of age, so I approve of the old man in whom there is some of the flavor of youth."[2]

Young ideas seem to defy both the past and the future and make a worthwhile today. "Old things are done away"[3] says the song. The past is gone and the future

193

may be uncertain, but what we do have is today, and "Our great resource," says Horatio W. Dresser, "is to ask what life is now,…"[4]

And to those who are younger, let's not try to be old too soon. Time will pass no faster just because we want it to. But, if our thoughts are always just for tomorrow, then today will pass us by. So whatever our age, wherever we are in life, today is the day to live and enjoy life. One of the greatest moments in our life might be today. Right now, today, this moment is what we have and we would do well to "look to this day." MARCH 12, 1972

The Passing of Time

We all know that time moves at a constant pace unaffected by mankind or anything we do. That is one of the surest facts we ever learn. Yet, time has a way of slipping by more rapidly when we need it most and dragging when we wish it to pass. Truly it is one of the phenomenons of this earth life, and perhaps even offers a unique insight into our joys and sorrows, our conquests and defeats, and our relationships with other people.

Time seems to race by when we are involved in something we enjoy: a child's playtime is never long enough, a summer vacation seems shorter than it really is, and a stimulating athletic encounter is always running out of time.

And the opposite is just as true: a particularly unpleasant homework assignment is always the longest, and waiting for someone when we're in a hurry makes the seconds seem like minutes.

But one of the most impressive ways the passing of time seems to manifest itself in our lives is in dealing with our loved ones. There is never time enough when

194

loved ones are together, for it passes too swiftly; and there is always too much time when they are apart, for it seems to drag. Time seems slowest when waiting for a doctor's diagnosis or a child's safe return, yet raising a son or daughter in a happy home can be the fastest twenty years in life.

It is interesting to note that the future always seems longer than the past. Two years ahead can seem like eternity, whereas in retrospect, two years just past can seem like a few fleeting hours.

But still the reality remains that time passes at a constant pace. Whether it appears to move slower or faster for us depends on our attitude and how we approach each day, in what we do with the time we have. We can waste it—slowly and sorrowfully, or we can experience new self-growth by seeking the good in life and perhaps gain a better understanding of time's passage and its effect on our lives.   MAY 5, 1974

"One To-day Is Worth
Two To-morrows"

There are many rewards in life worth planning and working for—education, careers, marriage, a family, and retirement, to name only a few. Nearly everyone plans for the future, and that is a good and necessary part of life. But, as in most things, moderation is important—an excess can be dangerous.

There are those, unfortunately, who are willing to sacrifice the present for the future. But if we do not care for today, tomorrow's hopes may never come, for the realities of the future lie in the accomplishments of the present—in the things we do just for today.

Benjamin Franklin observed that "One to-day is worth two to-morrows,"[5] and it has also been said that "We look backward too much and we look forward too much. Thus we miss the passing moment."[6]

To borrow the words of Kenneth Holmes, we might say to ourselves, "...I will try to live through this day only, and not tackle my whole life problem at once.... Just for today, I will try to strengthen my mind....I will learn something useful....Just for today,...I will do somebody a good turn,...[and] Just for today, I will be unafraid. Especially I will not be afraid to enjoy what is beautiful, and to believe that as I give to the world, so the world will give to me."[7]

According to one ancient writing:
Yesterday is but a Dream,
And Tomorrow is only a Vision:
But Today well-lived makes
Every Yesterday a Dream of Happiness,
And every Tomorrow a Vision of Hope.
Look well therefore to this day![8]

And the comfort in that advice is that we need do it "just for today."   NOVEMBER 5, 1972

"God Will Force No Man to Heaven"

Any man who has ever lost his freedom will readily agree that of all God's gifts, none is more precious than free agency. This freedom allows men to worship the Almighty in whatever manner they choose, and by the same token, to reject Him altogether. For as William Clegg wrote, "God will force no man to heaven."[9]

As we have pointed out before, this freedom carries a responsibility—a responsibility to understand the

196

wisdom, love and light which God provided to guide us through our earthly state. But the choice is still ours, as is the responsibility for the consequences.

Today is yet another day, a new opportunity to decide how we will apply our gift of freedom. It may be wasted, or it may be used to accomplish some lasting good. What is important to remember is that part of our life will be spent this day and permanently written in our life record. It can, therefore, be a day of gain or a day of loss. The choice is ours. Hopefully it will be a day of success, not failure; and happiness, not sorrow.

We should also realize that the price we pay for this day is premium and absolute. It is time! Once paid, it is irretrievable. So we must consider well what we purchase with our time. Let us so live that we will not regret the price we pay for each day.

We hold in our hands both the freedom and the time to do what we will with our lives. May we squander neither, but do as John Monsell suggests, and "Fight the good fight with all [our] might,…"[10]

MARCH 24, 1974

Hurrying Too Much and Accomplishing Too Little

At one time or another, we all find ourselves trying to do too much in too short a time. Sometimes it is inevitable, but most probably we let it happen more often than we would like to admit. The more we try to do, the less we seem to accomplish.

In this age of anxiety there is a greater need for us to stop and relax than ever before. Relaxation can replenish life; it is the means whereby we renew our physical and mental abilities. To relax does not mean we are wasting time. Quite the contrary. A few minutes of relaxation refreshes us, and we can return to our task able to do more and work better than if we had stayed on the job wearily fighting to the finish.

Most of us understand the need for relaxation, but we think of it only in terms of holidays and vacations. Where we fail is in not taking small breaks from our daily routine—just a momentary change of pace is all that is needed. The next time you need to get away from a perplexing problem, take a few moments and gaze out the window, or read a page or two from a good book, or lie down and day-dream for a few minutes; envision a physical landscape which is relaxing to you; listen to a favorite record; or just spend a few minutes with a favorite project or hobby. Even being alone for a few moments can be effective. You'll return to your task with renewed vigor and the capability of greater accomplishment.

Relaxation can be as simple as slowing down. A seventeenth-century philosopher once observed that there are those who "...devour more in one day than they can digest in a whole lifetime; they live in advance of pleasures, eat up the years beforehand, and by their hurry get through everything too soon."[11]

The next time the pace of life seems over-accelerated, and we suddenly realize we are hurrying too much and accomplishing too little, let us retreat for a few moments. One of the best ways we can refresh ourselves mentally, physically and spiritually is, as the song suggests, in a "Sweet Hour of Prayer."   MARCH 11, 1973

The Quiet Passing of Time

Time passes more quickly than we realize. But perhaps one of the pleasant blessings of life is the consistent, quiet passing of time. It doesn't happen all at once in one shocking moment. Unfortunately, there is a danger in this often hypnotic effect, for it lulls the senses, lulls us into a false feeling of security, and the belief that we have more time than we need to fulfill our objectives. This sense of timelessness was aptly expressed by Joseph Conrad: "I remember...the feeling that...I could last forever," he said, "outlast the sea, the earth, and all men."[12]

Some appropriate advice comes from Emerson. "Guard well your spare moments," he said. "They are like uncut diamonds. Discard them and their value will never be known. Improve them and they will become the brightest gems in a useful life."[13]

Time seems to pass most swiftly when we are away for a few days or weeks. But routine soon returns, and reminds us there are still the same number of hours in a day, the same number of days in a week, and the same number of weeks in a year. Its pace is constant—one which we can join in stride, but it will not stop or wait. One of the most difficult adjustments faced by returning prisoners of war, or anyone who has been away for some time, is the sudden realization that all has changed.

Let us not be fooled into thinking that there is always time enough to do what we need, or want, or should do. We need to be aware that there is a time for all things: "A time to be born and a time to die;...A time to weep and a time to laugh."[14] And if we remember that "To every thing there is a season, and a time to every purpose under heaven..."[14] then perhaps the quiet passing of time will not be so shocking.   MARCH 25, 1973

"...In Patience There Is Safety"

Last week we spoke of not wasting the time we have, of not idly dreaming about tomorrow at the expense of today.

Often we are led by a desire to have *now* that for which we hope. We too often find ourselves overly anxious for the things in life we want, which seem, at the time, most important. Young couples often go deeply in debt trying to start their life together at the same standard of living as their parents. Too many of us find it easier to say "charge it" rather than curb our desires with patience.

The lack of patience—the lack of self-control—is perhaps the greatest reason why people go too deeply in debt. "How poor are they who have not patience,"[15] wrote Shakespeare. There is nothing wrong with charge accounts and credit cards if one has the wisdom to use them wisely, the patience for clear thinking and controlled desires. And that holds true for all desires in life.

Those who are searching for a companion—especially the young—will find a great need for patience and self-control if they are to realize true happiness in life, if they are to remain virtuous and avoid the temptations of life. Sometimes this requires a great deal more effort than we suppose.

The lyrics of one of the songs the Mormon Tabernacle Choir sings tells of a couple who for seven years had been going together and then were separated for seven more, while he was "bound away 'cross the wide Missouri."[16] Often today even seven days can seem too long a time, and patience becomes difficult. We fail to realize, as George Horne expressed it, that "Patience strengthens the spirit, sweetens the temper,...restrains the hand, and tramples upon temptations."[17]

When we have the patience to do what is right, and in the proper course of time, we usually find our efforts turn out for the better. "Patience," says a Chinese proverb, "and the mulberry leaf becomes a silken gown."

So again, the future is important and we need to plan for it. But when our plans have been made, we need also to have the patience to make them come true. In the words of Josiah Holland, "There is no great achievement that is not the result of patient working and waiting "[18] "Patience—in patience there is safety."[19]   MARCH 19, 1972

The Challenge of Youth

One of the world's most vibrant and challenged groups is today's youth. According to the 1970 census, in the United States alone, nearly one half of the population is under twenty-five years of age. And more than half of that number—over fifty-six million—are between the ages of ten and twenty-five.

These young people, and other young people throughout the world, are developing the character of tomorrow's generation. They have a great challenge, which carries with it a great responsibility—a responsibility to all the inhabitants of the earth. Youth must not only seek new ideas, but seek also guidance from those who have acquired the wisdom of years.

And it is important that all young people everywhere know that they are children of a living God, of a Father who dwells in the heavens; who loves and trusts them with the great responsibilities that are theirs and offers them the direction they need to carry out their assignments.

Youth has always been challenged to improve old ways and find new methods, and the challenge has multiplied with each new generation. Today there are more opportunities of greater consequence than ever before. Tomorrow there will be even more.

Occasionally, young people are reckless in discharging their duties. They often procrastinate because to them there is always time enough tomorrow. Perhaps this is why our elders are with us to teach temperance and the virtue of being industrious.

Joseph Conrad said: "I remember my youth and the feeling that...I could last forever, outlast the sea, the earth, and all men."[20] In a way that is true. The eternities will make our youth last forever, but the clock of mortality ticks on and we must not let the opportunities of this age escape.

And so a tribute today to youth, to those who are meeting their challenge. May they always know that they are loved and needed. And to all who have passed through those cherished days, or who might still be there in one way or another, let us remember that there is nothing quite as sweet as youth.   JUNE 25, 1972

Suddenly We're Older

Nothing in life is quite so fleeting as the present moment. It quickly passes to become forever a memory. Thomas Aldrich wrote: "All the best sands of my life are somehow getting into the wrong end of the hourglass."[21] Indeed, life does pass more quickly than we think and suddenly we're older.

Cicero put the passing of time into better perspective when he likened the aging process to the passing of the seasons. And a wise man, he said, will no more lament his entrance into old age than a gardener will lament the arrival of the blooms and the fruit he has nurtured during spring and summer. The proper fruit to be gathered in the winter of our days, according to Cicero, is "to be able to look back with self-approving satisfaction on the happy and abundant produce of more active years."[22]

As we move toward the winter of our lives we must remember, as Paul said, that "...whatsoever a man soweth, that shall he also reap."[23] With the passing of each fleeting moment we build what has been called a "storehouse of memories." Each moment has the potential to become a treasured memory or an unwanted recollection. Both are indelibly etched into our memory banks.

As we grow older we make use of our memories to give us courage, to give us knowledge, to call to remembrance what has been learned or experienced, to renew our faith in the good things of life. How important it is then to fill our storehouse with the kind of memories we can benefit from, over and over again, through the years. And how important it is that we use each moment in a positive way, with as much concern for future memories as for the momentary pleasures of the present.

We have all forgotten more than we will ever remember. And though the years may take their toll on the physical body, the hope, the excitement, the exuberance of younger years can retain much of their vitality through warm, wonderful memories. Such is the message expressed in these lyrics:

> *Though Spring's warm rain has turned to sleet*
> *It still is Spring in memory—*
> *And though the years have slowed these feet,*
> *A youthful heart still runs to thee,*
> *Though suddenly we're older.* [24]   NOVEMBER 26, 1972

Time Is a Fluid Condition

Time is one of the more mysterious factors in our lives. Nothing is more constant yet so full of change, so scientific yet so subjective. Indeed, time is mysterious. When we are happy and enjoying ourselves, it seems to slip away; but when we are unhappy or lonely, time seems to almost struggle by, one second at a time.

Of course, we all know that time is a constant, that a second is always one sixtieth of a minute. What, then, makes the difference between those days when we look at the clock and wonder where the time went, and those days when we stare at the clock and wish the hour would pass?

Time does not change. It is our attitude that changes. We will find that time is good to us when we are good to time. We must make meaningful use of it. Meaning is derived from the goals we set, the habits we form, and the friendships we patiently develop. All of these require time. All of them use time in a meaningful way.

It is not always possible for us to control all of our time. There are those inevitable, lengthened moments when we must bear sad news, or when we are separated from loved ones, or when treasured plans are set aside. But even those moments can be meaningful if we are good to time: what better time is there to read a poem or to talk to God in prayer?

The story is told of a productive writer who travels widely. He always keeps a paper and pencil handy, and when others are wishing away minutes on long flights or agonizing over missed connections, he is making notes for his next book. He loves time. And time is good to him. To this man meaningful time is not just writing and traveling; it also includes teaching, raising a fine family, being active in church, business and government.

Inevitably time does "slip away." For some it simply disappears and leaves nothing. For others, when time is gone—monuments remain.   JULY 28, 1974

NOTES

CHAPTER 1

1 Ralph Waldo Emerson, *The Conduct of Life*

2 Charles de Secondat Montesquieu (1689-1755), French author

3 National Religious Press, cited in *The Treasure Chest*, edited by Charles L. Wallis

4 New Testament, John 13:17

5 William George Jordan, *The Majesty of Calmness: The Royal Road to Happiness*

6 Book of Mormon, 2 Nephi 2:15, 15

7 Old Testament, Psalms 23

8 New Testament, Matthew 6:24

9 William James, *Is Life Worth Living?*

10 New Testament, John 13:17

11 Samuel Butler, "Higgledy-Piggledy," *Note-Books*

12 Bertrand Russell, (1872-1974), English mathematician and philosopher

13 Washington Irving (1783-1859), American author

14 André Gide, *Journal of "The Counterfeiters,"* Second Notebook, August 1921

15 Song: "Let Nothing Ever Grieve Thee," text by Paul Flemming, music by Johannes Brahms, Op. 30

16 Marcus Aurelius, *Meditations*

17 Fulton J. Sheen, *Peace of Soul*

CHAPTER 2

1 Charles Angoff, Russian-born author

2 Old Testament, Proverbs 22:6

3 Ernie Ford, Honorary Chairman of Family Unity Month, April 1975

4 David O. McKay, L.D.S. Conference Address, April 4, 1964

5 Harold B. Lee, religious leader, The Church of Jesus Christ of Latter-day Saints (Mormon)

6 Dr. Neal A. Maxwell, *A Time to Choose*

7 William Lyon Phelps (1865-1943), American educator and literary critic

8 Wilferd A. Peterson, *The Art of Marriage*

9 Donald Culross Peattie (1898-1964), American author

10 Helen Steiner Rice, *What Is Marriage?*

11 Douglas Jerrold, *Douglas Jerrold's Wit: A Wedding-Gown*

12 Shakespeare, *III Henry VI*, Act IV, Sc. I, 1. 18

13 Hugh B. Brown, *You and Your Marriage*

14 Dr. Harry Emerson Fosdick, *Marriage*

15 Hymn: "Our God Is a God of Love," words by Delbert L. Stapley, Adapted by Robert Cundick

16 John Howard Payne, "Home, Sweet Home," from the first act of his opera, *Clari, The Maid of Milan*

17 Dr. John Henry Jowett (1864-1923), British-American clergyman

CHAPTER 3

1 New Testament, Matthew 19:14

2 Alan Beck, copyright 1950 by New England Mutual Life Insurance Company

3 New Testament, Matthew 18:3

4 Andrew Gillies (1870-1942), "Two Prayers," published in *Masterpieces of Religious Verse*, ed. by James Dalton Morrison, copyright by Harper & Row

5 Dr. Alexander Schreiner, Chief Organist, Salt Lake Mormon Tabernacle

6 Theodore Roosevelt, *The Honor of Homemaking*

7 Author unknown, quoted in *You and Your Marriage* by Hugh B. Brown

8 Attributed to Herbert Hoover, Thirty-first president of United States

9 New Testament, Matthew 19:14

10 Reverend Samuel Willard, in a Pastoral Letter to his congregation, May 1970

[11] Henry Ward Beecher, *Life Thoughts*

[12] Attributed to Abraham Lincoln, Sixteenth president of United States

[13] Walter Savage Landor (1775-1864), English author

[14] Dr. Charles Duncan McIver (1860-1906), Address given at North Carolina College for Women

[15] Song: "Nobody Knows De Trouble I've Seen," Author unknown, American Negro Spiritual

[16] Sydney Harris, "Parental Abilities and Limitations"

[17] William Aikman (1682-1731), Scottish portrait painter

[18] Drs. W. Dean Belnap and Glen C. Griffin, *About Life and Love*

[19] New Testament, Matthew 19:14

[20] Doctrine and Covenants 121:43

CHAPTER 4

[1] Chinese proverb

[2] Max Lerner, "The Gifts of the Magi," *Actions and Passions*

[3] Aristotle, *Politics*

[4] Mohandas K. Gandhi, *Non-Violence in Peace and War*

[5] Jean Anouilh, *Ardele* (1948)

[6] Rainer Maria Rilke, *Letters to a Young Poet*, May 14, 1904

[7] New Testament, Matthew 5:44

[8] Victor Hugo, *Les Miserables*

[9] Cicero, *Pro Archia Poeta*

[10] Samuel Johnson, *The Rambler*

[11] Rabindranath Tagore, *Stray Birds*

[12] Hegel, *Philosophy of History*, Introduction (1832)

[13] Pascal, *Pensées* (1670)

[14] Ralph Waldo Emerson, *Conduct of Life*, "Considerations by the Way" (1860)

[15] John Donne, *Devotions* (1624)

[16] Alexander Pope, *Essay on Criticism*, Part II

[17] Baltasar Gracián, *The Art of Worldly Wisdom*

[18] New Testament, Luke 6:37

[19] William Blake, "What God Is": *Jerusalem*

[20] Doctrine and Covenants 64:9

[21] New Testament, Matthew 11:6

[22] Shakespeare, *The Merchant of Venice*, Act IV

[23] Dorothy Sayers (1893-1957), English author

[24] Alexander Pope, *Essay on Criticism, Part II*

[25] Song: "Liberty," R. Paul Thompson

[26] Edward R. Murrow, December 31, 1955

[27] Thomas Paine, *The Rights of Man* (1791)

[28] Jonathan Swift, *Thought on Various Subjects* (1711)

CHAPTER 5

[1] Song: "The Gentle Way," dedicated to David O. McKay. Words by Edward L. Hart

[2] Antoine de Saint-Exupéry, *Wind, Sand and Stars*

[3] Dinah Maria Mulock Craik, *Friendship*

[4] Alfred Adler, *What Life Should Mean to Us*

[5] Ralph Waldo Emerson, "Friendship," *Essays: First Series* (1841)

[6] John Wesley, *Rules of Conduct*

[7] Richard L. Evans, *The Spoken Word*

[8] Henry Wadsworth Longfellow, *Kavanagh*

[9] Edward Everett Hale (1822-1909), Clergyman and writer

[10] John Stuart Mill, *On Liberty*

[11] A.M. Sullivan, quoted in *Capsuled Comments*, April 1973

[12] Ibid.

[13] Paul H. Dunn, L.D.S. Conference Address, April 6, 1973

[14] Kathy Brough, "Your Second Language"
[15] Ralph Waldo Emerson, "Behavior," *The Conduct of Life*

CHAPTER 6
[1] Doctrine and Covenants 130:20, 21
[2] Old Testament, Proverbs 29:18
[3] Earl Nightingale, "Private Versus Public," radio message
[4] New Testament, 1 Corinthians 3:16
[5] Ibid., 3:17
[6] Gus Turbeville, President, Emerson College, Boston. Address delivered September 12, 1973: "Victory Over Self," as president of Coker College, Hartsville, South Carolina
[7] Arabian proverb
[8] O. Henry, "Cupid a la Carte," *Heart of the West* (1907)
[9] Theognis, *Sententiae*
[10] Estelle R. Ries, Dietician
[11] David O. McKay, *Pathways to Happiness* (1957)
[12] Thomas Fuller (1608-1661), English clergyman and writer
[13] Maurice Maeterlinck, "Silence," *The Treasure of the Humble* (1896)
[14] Publilius Syrus, *Moral Sayings*, (1st c. B.C.)
[15] David Joseph Schwartz, *The Magic of Thinking Big*
[16] Marcus Aurelius, *Thoughts*, Book IV
[17] Thomas Carlyle, *Sartor Resartus* (1833-34)
[18] Thomas Carlyle, *Essays: The Opera*
[19] Doctrine and Covenants 25:12
[20] Leopold Stokowski, London-born musician
[21] Francisco A. De Icaza (1863-1924), *The Song By the Way*
[22] New Testament, Matthew 11:15
[23] Joyce Hifler, *Think on These Things* (1966), Doubleday & Co., Inc.
[24] Anne Frank, *The Diary of a Young Girl*
[25] William Wordsworth, *My Heart Leaps Up* (1807), *Magill's Quotations in Context*, Harper & Row
[26] John Keats, *Endymion*, Book 1
[27] Attributed to John Keats, as quoted in *Magill's Quotations in Context*, Harper & Row
[28] Sara Teasdale, *Night*
[29] Book of Mormon, I Nephi 17:36

CHAPTER 7
[1] Hugh B. Brown, religious leader, The Church of Jesus Christ of Latter-day Saints (Mormon)
[2] Alexis de Tocqueville, *La Démocratie en Amérique*, (1835)
[3] *The Christian Science Monitor: The Forum*, March 28, 1973
[4] New Testament, James 2:26
[5] Richard Cecil (1748-1777), English divine
[6] Book of Mormon, 2 Nephi 28:20,21
[7] Alfred Noyes (1880-1958), English poet and critic
[8] Morris West, from *The Devil's Advocate*
[9] Dr. Thomas F. O'Dea, from a talk delivered at the University of Utah, titled "The Protest of Youth: Revolution or Revelation"
[10] Alfred, Lord Tennyson, "Morte d'Arthur" (1842), *Magill's Quotations in Context*, Harper & Row
[11] Smiley Blanton, *Now or Never*
[12] Alexis Carrel, "Prayer Is Power," *Reader's Digest*, March 1941
[13] Song: "America, the Beautiful," Katherine Lee Bates
[14] New Testament, Matthew 21:22
[15] Abraham Lincoln, J.G. Holland's statement in *Life of Abraham Lincoln*
[16] Alfred, Lord Tennyson, *Idylls of the King*, "The Passing of Arthur" (1869)
[17] Mark Twain, *The Adventures of Huckleberry Finn*, "You Can't Pray a Lie," (1884)

[18] Brigham Young (1801-1877), American Mormon leader and colonizer
[19] Hymn: "O For a Closer Walk With God," words by William Cooper
[20] Beatrice Webb (1858-1943), English author
[21] Dr. Harry Emerson Fosdick, *On Being a Real Person*
[22] Marcus Aurelius, *Meditations*
[23] Attributed to Abraham Lincoln, Sixteenth president of United States
[24] Harry Edwards, *Intellectual Digest*, quoted in *Capsuled Comments*, September, 1973
[25] Hymn: "So Precious in the Sight of the Lord," words by Virginia Sapienza
[26] Shakespeare, *Hamlet*, Act III, Sc. 3
[27] New Testament, James 2:26
[28] Gordon B. Hinckley, *Deseret News*, Church Section, November 23, 1968
[29] Old Testament, Psalms 121:1
[30] Author unknown, quoted in *Reader's Digest*, September 1949
[31] Doctrine and Covenants 90:24
[32] Kahlil Gibran, *The Prophet*

CHAPTER 8

[1] New Testament, Matthew 16:24; Mark 8:34; Luke 9:59
[2] Pearl of Great Price, Moses 1:39
[3] New Testament, John 17:3
[4] J. Reuben Clark, Jr., Address delivered at Brigham Young University December 11, 1951
[5] New Testament, John 1:1,4-5
[6] Ibid., 8:12
[7] Old Testament, Psalms 112:4
[8] Harold B. Lee, An Easter Message for TV, presented with the Mormon Tabernacle Choir, April 1973
[9] New Testament, John 14:27
[10] Accredited to Thomas A. Edison in *There Is No Unanswerable Prayer*, by Margaret Blair Johnstone
[11] New Testament, John 14:27
[12] Joseph Conrad, prologue to Part 1, *Under Western Eyes* (1911)
[13] La Rochefoucauld, *Maximes Supprémées*
[14] Ralph Waldo Emerson, *Essays*, "Of Self-Reliance"
[15] New Testament, Philippians 4:7
[16] Hymn: "Lead, Kindly Light," Rev. John H. Newman
[17] Dr. Glen C. Griffin, *About Life and Love*
[18] New Testament, Luke Ch. 24
[19] Richard L. Evans, Address at the funeral service for Jessie Evans Smith, August 5, 1971
[20] New Testament, John 11:25, 26

CHAPTER 9

[1] Author unknown
[2] John Foster Dulles (1888-1959), U.S. Secretary of State
[3] David O. McKay, CBS Church of the Air address, December 19, 1943
[4] New Testament, Hebrews 11:1 (Inspired Version)
[5] Ralph Waldo Emerson (1803-1882), American poet, essayist, philosopher
[6] Song: "Hatikva," words adapted by L.C. Zucker
[7] Thales as quoted by Epictetus, *Fragment*
[8] Lyndon B. Johnson (1908-1973), Thirty-sixth president of United States
[9] Floyd H. Ross and Tynette Hills, *The Great Religions by Which Men Live*
[10] Wilferd A. Peterson, *The Art of Hope*
[11] Dr. Harry Emerson Fosdick, American theologian and author
[12] Ralph Waldo Trine, *In Tune With the Infinite*
[13] Hymn: "O My Father," words by Eliza R. Snow
[14] New Testament, Matthew 17:20
[15] Song: "Anyone Can Move a Mountain," words by Johnny Marks

[16] Song: "The Windows of the World," words by Hal David
[17] George Washington, *Remark*, during discussion, Constitutional Convention
[18] George Washington, *Morals Maxims: Virtue and Vice*
[19] James A. Garfield, Address, April 1865
[20] Warren G. Harding, Speech, Boston, May 1920

CHAPTER 10
[1] Brigham Young, *Journal of Discourses*, 10:221
[2] Old Testament, Proverbs 4:7
[3] Harold B. Lee, L.D.S. Conference Address, October 7, 1972
[4] William Cowper, *God Moves in a Mysterious Way*
[5] Song: "Not Now, But in the Coming Years," Maxwell N. Cornelius, D.D. (Music by James McGranahan)
[6] Hymn: "Come, Come, Ye Saints," words by William Clayton
[7] George Frederic Handel, *The Messiah* (1741)
[8] Attributed to Abraham Lincoln, Sixteenth president of United States
[9] William Henry Davies, "Leisure," *Songs of Joy* (1911)
[10] Old Testament, Psalms 19:1
[11] Ibid., 8:4
[12] Song: "Gentle Annie," Stephen Foster
[13] George Spring Merriam, *A Living Faith*
[14] George Frederic Handel, *Their Bodies Are Buried in Peace* (See also *Apocrapha: Ecclesiasticus* 44:14)

CHAPTER 11
[1] Maltbie Babcock, quoted in *The Treasure Chest*, edited by Charles L. Wallis, Harper & Row
[2] Accredited to Bishop Brooke Foss Westcott (1825-1901), English prelate
[3] Henry Ward Beecher, *Life Thoughts*
[4] William Hersey Davis, quoted in *The Treasure Chest*, edited by Charles L. Wallis, Harper & Row
[5] Joel Hawes, quoted in *The Treasure Chest*, edited by Charles L. Wallis, Harper & Row
[6] Book of Mormon, 2 Nephi 2:11, 15
[7] Gus Turbeville, President, Emerson College, Boston. Address delivered September 12, 1973: "Victory Over Self" as President, Coker College, Hartsville, South Carolina
[8] William George Jordan, *The Kingship of Self-Control*
[9] Anthony Ashley Cooper, Earl of Shaftesbury
[10] Lord Chesterfield (1694-1773), English statesman and author
[11] Baltasar Gracian, *The Art of Worldly Wisdom*
[12] Harold B. Lee, L.D.S. Area Conference, Mexico City, August 28, 1972
[13] Theodore E. Curtis, *Lean On My Ample Arm*
[14] Attributed to Mohandas K. Gandhi (1869-1948), Hindu leader
[15] Dr. Neal A. Maxwell, *A Time to Choose*
[16] Mark E. Petersen, *Drugs, Drinks, and Morals*
[17] Song: "Fight the Good Fight," words by J.S.B. Monsell (1863)
[18] W.M. Thackery, *The Virginians* (1858)
[19] Walter Bagehot, *Biographical Studies* (1881)
[20] New Testament, Matthew 6:13
[21] Ibid., 1 Corinthians 10:13
[22] George Washington, *Morals Maxims: Virtue and Vice*
[23] New Testament, Matthew 26:41
[24] Shakespeare, *Hamlet*, Act I, Sc. 3
[25] Thomas Carlyle (1795-1881), Scottish-born English author

CHAPTER 12
[1] New Testament, Matthew 7:1
[2] Accredited to Bishop Brooke Foss Westcott (1825-1901, English prelate

[3] Henri-Frederic Amiel, *Journal,* December 1859
[4] Old Testament, Leviticus 19:18
[5] Seneca, *Epistulae ad Licilium*
[6] William George Jordan, *The Kingship of Self-Control*
[7] John Locke (1632-1704), English philosopher
[8] Aristotle, *Nicomachean Ethics*
[9] Paraphrased from *The Kingship of Self-Control,* by William George Jordan
[10] Vashnie Young, author and advertising executive
[11] Ralph Waldo Emerson, *Self-Reliance*
[12] Baltasar Gracian, *The Art of Worldly Wisdom*
[13] Author unknown
[14] Shakespeare, *Hamlet,* Act I, Sc. 3
[15] New Testament, Matthew 22:36-39
[16] Eric Hoffer, *The Passionate State of Mind* (1954), Harper & Row
[17] David Seabury. *The Art of Selfishness,* Introduction, Simon & Schuster, Inc.
[18] Song: "There Is a Balm in Gilead," music by William L. Dawson, words from scripture (see Old Testament, Jeremiah 8:22)
[19] Doctrine and Covenants 101:37
[20] New Testament, Matthew 16:26
[21] Nathaniel Branden, *The Psychology Of Self-Esteem* (1969), Nash Publ. Corp.
[22] Aldous Huxley (1894-1963), English novelist, essayist, satirist
[23] Ugo Betti, *The Inquiry*
[24] Aesop, *The Fox and the Mask*
[25] Shakespeare, *Hamlet,* Act I, Sc. 3
[26] Dr. Hans Selye, *The Stress of Life*
[27] Ralph Waldo Emerson, *Letters and Social Aims: Progress of Culture*
[28] Old Testament, Proverbs 23:7
[29] Joyce Hifler, *Think on These Things,* (1966), Doubleday & Co., Inc.
[30] George Bernard Shaw, *An Unsocial Socialist*
[31] Horace Mann (1796-1859), American educator
[32] New Testament, Philippians 4:8

CHAPTER 13
[1] Quoted in a book, *A More Excellent Way,* by Dr. Neal A. Maxwell
[2] Georg Brandes, Danish critic and writer
[3] Old Testament, Psalms 16:1
[4] Ralph Waldo Emerson, *Self-Reliance*
[5] Henry Wadsworth Longfellow (1807-1822), American poet
[6] Martin Luther's statement to the interrogator of Emperor Charles V, *Diet of Worms,* April 18, 1521
[7] Confucius, as quoted in *International Dictionary of Thoughts,* Doubleday & Co., Inc.
[8] John Ruskin, *Modern Painters*
[9] Jawaharlal Nehru (1889-1964), Indian statesman
[10] Doctrine and Covenants 112:10
[11] St. Bernard of Clairvaux (1091-1153), French ecclesiastic
[12] Sir John Buchan (1875-1940), Scottish author
[13] Author unknown
[14] John F. Kennedy, *Profiles in Courage*
[15] Alexander Pope, *Essay on Criticism, Part II*
[16] William George Jordan, *The Majesty of Calmness*
[17] Capt. Larry Chesley speaking of Maj. Jay C. Hess
[18] Attributed to Plato
[19] Doctrine and Covenants 88:124
[20] Ibid., 42:42
[21] Hymn: "God of Our Fathers, Whose Almighty Hand," words by Daniel C. Roberts
[22] Hymn: "We Are Sowing," Author unknown

[23] Nathan Eldon Tanner, religious leader, The Church of Jesus Christ of Latter-day Saints (Mormon)
[24] New Testament, Matthew 5:16
[25] Hymn: "Come, Let Us Anew," words by Charles Wesley

CHAPTER 14
[1] Sydney Justin Harris, American newspaper columnist
[2] Thomas Carlyle (1795-1881), Scottish-born English author
[3] Maurice Valency, introduction to *Jean Giraudoux: Four Plays* (1958)
[4] John Heron, *The Royal Bank of Canada Monthly Letter*, Vol. 55, No. 1
[5] Accredited to Thomas Carlyle
[6] William George Jordan, *The Kingship of Self-Control*
[7] Jack Anderson, speech delivered in Park City, Utah, 1973, at the Utah Broadcasters Association Convention
[8] Oliver Cromwell (1599-1658), English statesman
[9] Charles Kingsley (1819-75), English clergyman and novelist
[10] Henry Van Dyke, *The Zest of Life*
[11] Hymn: "Though Deepening Trials," words by Eliza R. Snow
[12] Hymn: "Lift Thine Eyes to the Mountains," Felix Mendelssohn
[13] John Heron, *The Royal Bank of Canada Monthly Letter*, Vol. 55, No. 11
[14] Marvin J. Ashton, L.D.S. Conference Address, October 1974
[15] Paul H. Dunn, *Anxiously Engaged*
[16] Ralph Waldo Emerson, *Destiny*
[17] Henry Wadsworth Longfellow, *Hyperion*, Book I
[18] Ralph Waldo Emerson, *Uncollected Lectures: Public and Private Education*
[19] Henry Ward Beecher, *Life Thoughts*
[20] Irving Berlin, *Theatre Arts*, February 1958
[21] Josiah Gilbert Holland (1819-81), American author, quoted in *New Dictionary of Thoughts*
[22] Robert Browning, *Andrea del Sarto*

CHAPTER 15
[1] Robert Browning Hamilton, "Along the Road"
[2] Mark Twain (1835-1910), American writer and humorist
[3] Marcus Aurelius, *Thoughts*, Book V
[4] Seneca, *Epistle to Lucilius*
[5] John Heron, *The Royal Bank of Canada Monthly Letter*, Vol.54, No. 1
[6] Hymn: "Lean On My Ample Arm" Theodore E. Curtis
[7] Song: "Hard Times, Come Again No More," Stephen C. Foster
[8] Harold B. Walker, *Power to Manage Yourself*
[9] Dr. Harry Emerson Fosdick, *On Being a Real Person: Mastering Depression*
[10] Hymn: "When Upon Life's Billows," Rev. J. Oatman, Jr.
[11] Henry W. Longfellow, *Hyperion*, *III*
[12] Hymn: "Cast Thy Burden Upon the Lord," Felix Mendelssohn
[13] David O. McKay, *Gospel Ideals*
[14] Theodore Roosevelt, speech made before the Hamilton Club, Chicago, April 10, 1899
[15] Epictetus, *Discourses* Book 1
[16] R.G. Ingersoll, *The Declaration of Independence*
[17] Franklin D. Roosevelt, message for Jefferson Day, April 13, 1945
[18] Saint-Exupéry, *Wind, Sand, and Stars*, (1939)
[19] Samuel Johnson, *The Rambler*
[20] Mahatma Gandhi (1869-1948), Hindu leader
[21] Marie Currie (1867-1934), Polish-born physicist and chemist
[22] Epictetus, *Discourses*

CHAPTER 16
[1] Thomas Carlyle, *Past and Present: Labour*

211

[2] Mark E. Petersen, L.D.S. Conference Address, October 7, 1973
[3] New Testament, Matthew 11:28-30
[4] Hymn: "Sweet Is the Work, My God, My King," Isaac Watts
[5] Charles Kingsley, *Town and Country Sermons*
[6] New Testament, James 2:20
[7] Jane Ellice Hopkins, *Work Amongst Working Men*
[8] Michelangelo (1475-1564), Italian sculptor, painter, architect and poet of Renaissance
[9] Dr. Frank Crane, *The Looking Glass*
[10] Joseph Conrad (1857-1924), Polish-born English novelist
[11] Niccolo Machiavelli (1469-1527), Italian statesman and political philosopher
[12] Theodore Roosevelt (1858-1919), Twenty-sixth president of United States
[13] John Heywood, *Proverbs*
[14] Hymn: "Come, Come, Ye Saints," words by William Clayton
[15] Brigham Young, *Journal of Discourses*, 5:481
[16] Ralph Waldo Emerson, *Conduct of Life: Worship*
[17] Doctrine and Covenants 130:20, 21
[18] Dr. Leonard L. Lovshin
[19] Sydney Harris, American newspaper columnist
[20] Song: "Come, Listen to a Prophet's Voice," Joseph J. Daynes
[21] Sophocles, *Electra* (c. 418-14 B.C.)
[22] John Collins (1848-1908), English literary critic
[23] New Testament, Matthew 7:7
[24] Mahatma Gandhi (1869-1948), Hindu leader

CHAPTER 17
[1] Old Testament, Ecclesiastes 3:1, 2
[2] Cicero, *De Senectut*, Ch. XI, Sec. 38
[3] Leroy J. Robertson, *Oratorio: Old Things Are Done Away*
[4] Horatio Willis Dresser (1866-1954), American editor, author and philosopher
[5] Benjamin Franklin, *Poor Richard*
[6] William Lyon Phelps, *Essays on Things*
[7] Kenneth L. Holmes, *Just for Today*
[8] *The Salutation of the Dawn*, based on the Sanskrit
[9] Song: "Know This, That Every Soul Is Free," William C. Clegg
[10] Song: "Fight the Good Fight," words by J.S.B. Monsell
[11] Baltasar Gracian, *The Art of Worldly Wisdom*
[12] Joseph Conrad, *Youth* (1903)
[13] Attributed to Ralph Waldo Emerson
[14] Old Testament, Ecclesiastes 3:1-4
[15] Shakespeare, *Othello*, Act II, Sc. 3
[16] Song: "Shenandoah," early American barge song
[17] George Horne (1730-92), English bishop
[18] Josiah G. Holland (1819-81), American author
[19] Laboulaye, *Abdallah*, Ch. 20
[20] Joseph Conrad, *Youth* (1903)
[21] Thomas Bailey Aldrich, "Leaves From a Notebook," *Ponkapog Papers*
[22] Cicero, *Old Age*
[23] New Testament, Galations 6:7
[24] Lyrics from the song: "Suddenly You're Older," L. Clair Likes, music: Robert F. Brunner, *Brunner Music Publishing Co.*

INDEX

INDEX

213

217